Collections from an Aspen Chef

Collections from an Aspen Chef

Favorite recipes with options to accommodate your dietary preferences. Use them as is, or easily modify into gluten free, dairy free or vegan.

Written & Illustrated by Cindy Rogers

Treedogpress Studio

Aspen, Colorado

Copyright © 2015, ©2017 by Cindy Rogers/Treedogpress Studio, LLC

All Rights Reserved

No part of this publication may be reproduced or transmitted in any form or by any means, electronic or mechanical, including photocopying, recording or any other information storage and retrieval system, without the written permission of the author or publisher.

Collections from an Aspen Chef/Cindy Rogers
Written by Cindy Rogers
Design & Illustrations by Cindy Rogers

Author's photo by Mark Batmale

Hard cover - ISBN - 978-0-9969821-3-9
Paperback - ISBN - 978-0-9969821-4-6
eBook - ISBN - 978-0-9969821-2-2

Typeface - Century Gothic

Printed by Lightning Source/Ingram Spark
In the United States of America

Published by Treedogpress Studio, LLC
P.O. Box 125, Woody Creek, CO 81656
www.collectionsfromanaspenchef.com

Aspen, Colorado

Dedicated to my late little bro' David.
Out of necessity, I learned how to cook at the age of 10;
David never complained about my experiments and mishaps.
He was my biggest fan.

And also dedicated to the late, wonderful
Bonnie Rayburn, who ignited my passion for cooking!
She was an inspiration in the kitchen and in life.

Collections from an Aspen Chef
Favorite recipes with options to accommodate your dietary preferences

Disclaimer: The material in this cookbook is for general information purposes only and does not provide medical advice. This book is intended only as an informative guide to communicate general information about food choices and preparation. The information provided in this book may be helpful in implementing healthy food options; however, it is in no way intended to be a substitute for medical advice, diagnosis or treatment. If you require a medical diagnosis or prescription, or if you are contemplating any major dietary change, consult a qualified health-care provider prior to implementation. Never rely on the content of this, or any, cookbook in place of seeking professional medical advice, or delay seeking professional medical care. All material presented in this book is accurate to the best knowledge of the Author. By using this book, readers agree to the responsibility of knowing their own dietary limitations and understand that some ingredients in this book may be harmful to some people.

The author and publisher disclaim all liability in connection with the use of this book. The names and identifying details of people associated with events described in this book have been changed. Any similarity to actual persons is coincidental. All trademarks and brands referenced in the cookbook are the property of their respective owners, and no claim is made to them nor benefit received from their appearance or endorsement in this cookbook.

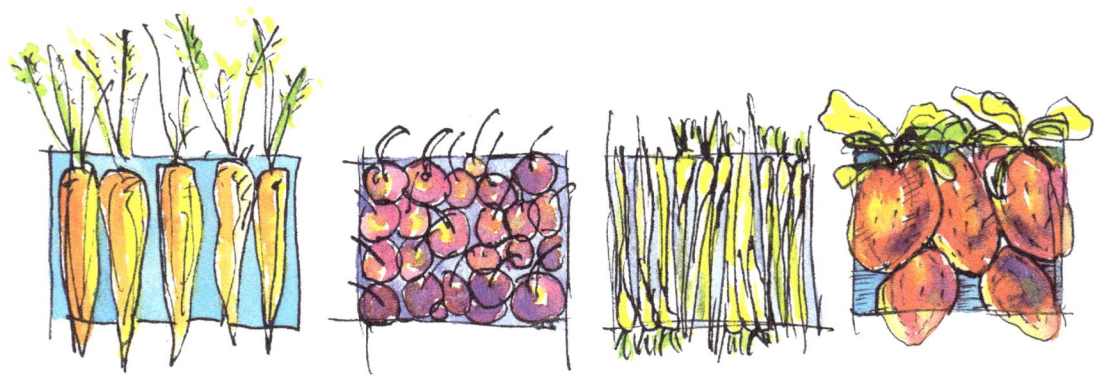

Collections from an Aspen Chef

Favorite recipes with options to accommodate your dietary preferences

CONTENTS:

Introduction	6 - 7
Pantry	8 - 13
Kitchen Essentials	14 - 15
Appetizers	16 - 31
Salads & Dressings	32 - 45
Soups	46 - 63
Side Dishes	64 - 81
Mexican & Italian	82 - 93
Canned Favorites	94 - 101
Lamb, Beef, Pork, Poultry & Fish	102 - 125
Desserts	126 - 151
Cookies & Holiday Egg Nog	152 - 167
Breakfast Yummies	168 - 180
Glossary	181 - 185
Index	186 - 191
Acknowledgments	192 - 193

GF = Gluten Free ～ DF = Dairy Free ～ VG = Vegan ～ ❄ = Freezes Well

Collections from an Aspen Chef
Favorite recipes with options to accommodate your dietary preferences

Introduction

Understanding the alchemy of food has been an ongoing fascination of mine. At the age of ten, I took on the responsibilities of grocery shopping and cooking for my beloved younger brother and myself. This led to a lot of experiments – some successful, some never to be repeated. All of this started me down the path to the way I think about food today. Mixing, adding, and adjusting recipes is the inspiration for creating delightful meals, with memorable flavor as my primary goal!

In the late '80s I started cooking for Bonnie Rayburn, of "Bonnie's" restaurant, which is located at 10,000 feet on the Aspen Mountain ski area. Bonnie ignited my passion and drive to create inviting, flavorful food. She instilled a confidence in me in the kitchen that began my career as a private chef in Aspen thirty years ago. Along the way I learned to accommodate a number of different and challenging menu requirements. Some due to dietary restrictions, others to severe allergies, and some to taste preferences; including no gluten, eggs, dairy and in some cases nothing with a face (vegan). In addition to my own severe allergic reactions to certain foods - learning to adapt my cooking style has been a never-ending education.

From the age of twelve I was plagued with migraines and ulcers. I didn't realize that food allergies and stress were the triggers. Food allergies were not a commonly discussed problem back in the '70s, '80s or even '90s. They weren't on most doctors' radar. My allergies along with food intolerances were depleting my system and compounding my health issues. By the age of forty I was tired of being sick. Mainstream allergists weren't offering a solution. My path crossed with an amazing allergy doctor with training in both Eastern and Western philosophies of medicine. He performed a series of tests for food reactions. As a result, he gave me a long list of foods to eliminate from my diet; including those producing the most severe reactions - shellfish, dairy, wheat, rosemary and coffee. As difficult as the elimination diet was, I began to feel better in less than three weeks. When I tried to add some of these foods back into my diet, I became violently ill. So began my journey to modify recipes to suit my dietary needs and still scratch that "comfort food itch".

Aspen is not your typical provincial small town. Besides its spectacular beauty, cultural attractions, and outdoor adventures, it's a unique place which draws people who have sophisticated palates. Visitors come here from all over the world. Aspen is an amazing and challenging place to be a private chef! My clients expect delicious five-star meals served in the privacy of their homes. Along with a tasty meal, there are always special requests for dairy free, gluten free and vegan alternatives. I've learned to have a variety of dishes on the menu that will accommodate everyone's needs.

Collections from an Aspen Chef
Favorite recipes with options to accommodate your dietary preferences

This book has been in the making for over ten years. During that time I've continued experimenting and rewriting recipes as new ingredients geared towards food allergies appeared on grocery shelves. This cookbook is foremost about tasty recipes along with healthy options to modify for your dietary needs - flavor is essential! This book is not specifically gluten free, dairy free or vegan; I offer a wide variety of dishes that will appeal to everyone.

I am sharing recipes in this book that my clients and I have enjoyed during my career. Even if you don't have food allergies, your guests may have dietary restrictions. If they do, the one thing that will make them happy is to have something on the table that works for them. This can be difficult to accomplish if you have never had to think about food allergies or restrictions. Most of my recipes have a note at the top right of the page, or to the right of each recipe to identify whether it's gluten free **(GF)**, dairy free **(DF)**, or vegan **(VG)**. Along with sidebars to help you modify the ingredients to suit your needs. There are a few recipes without any suggestions; I left these in for those of you who don't have any dietary preferences. I hope some of these recipes can help familiarize you with how easy it is to adjust recipes into gluten free, dairy free or vegan.

Out of respect for the privacy of all the people I've cooked for, I cannot name-drop any clients or reveal any experiences from time spent in their kitchens. There are some unforgettable and hilarious stories that regretfully can't be told…You can leave that up to your imagination.

"Collections from an Aspen Chef" will introduce you to some new recipes, some old familiar favorites and a few treasures from friends and family that can be adapted to work for everyone at the table.

Enjoy,
Cindy Rogers

Collections from an Aspen Chef
Favorite recipes with options to accommodate your dietary preferences

Pantry

When stocking my pantry I always look for organic and Non GMO ingredients. And if possible, I do my produce shopping at local farmers markets. If you are shopping for gluten free, dairy free or vegan, always look at the labels. Gluten, dairy and animal products can be hidden in ingredient lists under names you might not be aware of.

Shopping for (DF) non-dairy products – beware of casein, caseinates, whey, (these are milk-derived proteins), rennet, and of course all milks and cheeses, caramel coloring, lactose and lactose starters (some are dairy free, lactose is generally a sugar extracted from milk). **EGGS are NOT dairy!** A dairy product is a food produced from the milk of lactating mammals.

Shopping for (GF) gluten free products - always check the label for gluten free! Sources of gluten are found in wheat, barley, rye, malt and Brewer's yeast. Be careful of maltodextrin. It's derived from starch, usually corn, but sometimes wheat. Commercial French fries and grated cheese can be coated in flour to keep them from sticking. Check the ingredients list for caramel, it can be made with wheat and dairy. Make sure oats are labeled gluten free. Some are made in a facility that processes wheat.

Shopping for (VG) vegan products - animal products can be hidden in the form of gelatin, which is derived from the skins or bones of animals. Glycerin, lactic acid and steric acid can also be produced from slaughterhouse fat, but they could also be vegan. Lard is derived from animal fat. Mayonnaise and some pastas contain eggs. Also check for dairy products in the ingredients.

Abbreviation table

DF = dairy free
GF = gluten free
VG = vegan
❄ = freezes well
C = cup
T = tablespoon
tsp = teaspoon
S & P = kosher salt and fresh cracked black pepper to taste
gal = gallon
lb = pound
oz = ounce
qt = quart
.66 oz pkg – the size of packaged fresh herbs widely found in the produce section of the grocery store

Collections from an Aspen Chef
Favorite recipes with options to accommodate your dietary preferences

My Spice Drawer
I am severely allergic to rosemary, so you won't find it in this list. However it is usually part of a good spice collection. Most spices I order online at Penzeys.com.

Ancho chili powder
Bay leaves
Basil leaves
Cajun blackening seasoning (recipe found on pg. 89)
Cardamom – ground
Cayenne pepper
Chili powder - online @ El Potrero Trading Post
Cinnamon powder and sticks
Coriander – ground and seeds
Crushed red pepper
Cumin – ground and seeds
Curry powder
Fenugreek
Garlic powder
Ginger – ground
Juniper berries
Kosher salt
Maldon® salt - at specialty stores
Marjoram leaves
Mustard seeds – whole
Mustard, dry (Coleman's® brand)
Nutmeg - ground
Oregano leaves
Onion powder
Paprika
Pepper - black pepper (ground and peppercorns), white pepper and lemon pepper
Sage - leaves
Tony Chachere's® Creole Seasoning - at your local grocery store
Thyme
Turmeric
Turmeric salt – Gourmet Hawaiian® Salt (I get this from Hawaii – it's amazing)
Vanilla extract

Disclaimer: All trademarks and brands referenced in "Collections from an Aspen Chef" are the property of their respective owners, and no claim is made to them nor benefit received from their appearance or endorsement in this cookbook.

Collections from an Aspen Chef
Favorite recipes with options to accommodate your dietary preferences

My Faves!

These are the main ingredients you will find stocked in my pantry. Most of them you can find at grocery stores, some are found in Asian grocery stores, Trader Joe's®, and WHOLE FOODS® . Always check and recheck your labels, the manufacturers sometimes change their recipes.

Better Than Bouillon® Organic Chicken base (organic has no dairy, but their regular chicken base does contain dairy in the form of whey). This comes in a paste form that will hold in your refrigerator for months. It's easy to use and the flavor is good.

Better Than Bouillon® Vegetable base - this is a good vegan base, it comes in a paste form that will hold in your refrigerator for months. It's easy to use and I like the flavor.

Coconut oil - when I talk about coconut oil, I'm usually referring to a brand that doesn't smell or taste like coconut. My favorite two brands are LouAna® coconut oil and Spectrum® organic coconut oil - refined (unrefined will taste and smell like coconut).

Coconut milk in a carton – At the time of publishing this cookbook, in my opinion, So Delicious® Coconut Milk (in a carton) is the only unflavored coconut milk that comes the closest to replacing cow's milk. This is my personal preference for a non-dairy substitute. There is a big difference between coconut milk in a can versus in a carton.

Coconut milk in the can – Canned coconut milk has a distinctive coconut flavor with a high sugar and fat content. It's great for curries and desserts. I prefer Thai Kitchen® unsweetened coconut milk.

Earth Balance® – non-dairy vegan butter substitutes - vegan shortening and the original buttery spread contain soy, they also make a soy-free version.

JUST MACNUTS BUTTA'®, Raw & Roasted – Macadamia nut butter. Buy in Hawaii, or find online.

Parmigiano Reggiano – is the only kind of Parmesan cheese I use.

Thai Kitchen® red curry paste – I prefer this brand because it is vegan and contains no shellfish.

Condiments, Oils, Vinegars, Beans & Grains
Condiments -
Bragg® Liquid Aminos – GF alternative to soy sauce (has soy)
Chinese black vinegar – found in Asian stores

Collections from an Aspen Chef
Favorite recipes with options to accommodate your dietary preferences

Creole mustard, Zatars® - found in specialty stores
Dijon mustard - Grey Poupon®
Fish sauce – Tiparos®
Hoisin sauce
Honey – local if possible
Mirin – a low-alcohol rice wine that is made by fermenting freshly steamed rice.
Pomegranate molasses, Indo European® - found in Asian and specialty stores
Tabasco®
Tamari – GF alternative to soy sauce (has soy)
Worcestershire® sauce - Lee & Perrins® is GF, (beware, it has anchovies)

Oils –
Canola oil
Coconut oil - Spectrum® organic, refined or LouAna®
Extra virgin olive oil – a good quality brand
Pam® - nonstick cooking spray
Sesame oil

Vinegars -
Apple cider vinegar
Balsamic vinegar – red and white
Champagne vinegar
Fig or Blackberry Balsamic Vinegar - Westwood Farms®
Rice wine vinegar - Marukan® Seasoned Gourmet
Red wine vinegar
White vinegar

Canned Goods –
100% pure pumpkin puree – for baking
Chipotle peppers canned in Adobo sauce – La Costena®
Hatch® green chile
Herdez® – Salsa Casera and Salsa Verde
Tomatoes – diced, sauce and paste (plain)

Beans, Grains & Pastas –
Adzuki beans
Black eyed peas
Chick peas (garbanzo beans)
Mung beans
Pinto beans

Collections from an Aspen Chef
Favorite recipes with options to accommodate your dietary preferences

Lentils
Jasmine rice
Quinoa - red and traditional
Rice noodles – thick (Pad Thai style)
Spring roll rice sheets – round sheets (the rose labeled seems to be the best quality)
Wheat berries
Wild rice
Tinkyada® Brown Rice Pasta
Le Veneziane® Corn Pasta
Explore Asian®, Authentic cuisine - Organic Edamame & Mung Bean Fettuccine - (soy)

Baking Pantry -
Almond meal – ground
Arrowroot powder
Baking powder
Baking soda
Brown sugar
Chocolate bars, semi-sweet & unsweetened – Scharffen Berger® is my favorite
Chocolate bar, bittersweet - Green & Blacks® (it's dairy free)
Chocolate chips – Trader Joes® makes dairy free chips
Cocoa powder, unsweetened
Coconut flakes – shredded and large-flaked
Corn starch - (check label to see if it was made in a GF facility)
Corn meal - Bob's Red Mill® fine and medium grit
Cream of tarter
Dehydrated egg whites - DEB EL® or you can get a different brand at King Arthur Flour®
Flaxseed meal – ground (store in the refrigerator)
Flour – King Arthur Flour® Unbleached All-Purpose Flour
Liquid pectin pouches
Oats – rolled (check label to see if it was made in a GF facility)
Potato starch
Powdered sugar
Rice flour – both brown and white
SAF-Instant® yeast – store in the refrigerator (I order online from King Arthur Flour®)
Sugar
Tapioca flour - Bob's Red Mill®
Xanthan gum - Bob's Red Mill®

Collections from an Aspen Chef
Favorite recipes with options to accommodate your dietary preferences

U.S Weights & Measures
1 pinch = less than ⅛ tsp - dry
1 dash = 3 drops to ¼ tsp - liquid
1 T = 3 tsp = .5 oz
5 T + 1 tsp = ⅓ C
⅛ C = 1 oz = 2 T = 6 tsp
¼ C = 2 oz = 4 T = 12 tsp
½ C = 4 oz = 8 T = 24 tsp
⅔ C = 5 oz = 11 T = 32 tsp
¾ C = 6 oz = 12 T = 36 tsp
1 C = 8 oz = ½ pint = 16 T
2 C = 16 oz = 1 pint = 1 lb
4 C = 32 oz = 2 pints = 1 qt
16 C = 4 qts = 1 gal

Safe Minimum Cooking Temperatures
Beef, Veal & Lamb - rare 125°, medium rare 130°, medium 145°

Turkey, Chicken, Duck or Goose - 165°

Pork & Ham - 145°

Shrimp, Lobster & Crabs - Cook until flesh is pearly and opaque

Clams, Oysters & Mussels - Cook until shell opens during cooking

Scallops - Cook until flesh is milky white or opaque and firm

Collections from an Aspen Chef
Favorite recipes with options to accommodate your dietary preferences

Kitchen Essentials – Appliances, Pots & Pans, Knives & Tools

I've spent my years as a chef building up a small collection of tools and equipment I call my essentials. These essentials are indispensable to me. The more of these you have the easier your time in the kitchen will be.

Appliances

Blender – an upright blender with a fixed blade, used to chop, mix and puree.

Electric Hand Mixer - a handheld electric mixer that comes with beater attachments.

Food Processor - Cuisinart® is my brand of choice. A kitchen appliance similar to a blender only it has interchangeable blades and discs, instead of a fixed blade. Uses little or no liquid to operate.

Immersion Blender or Soup Wand – an appliance used to blend or purée food in the containers they are prepared in.

Seal-A-Meal® or FoodSaver® - vacuum sealer appliances used to put away and freeze food, keeping food fresh longer and extending the shelf life.

Stand Mixer - KitchenAid® is my brand of choice – a kitchen appliance for all your baking needs. It comes with a detachable paddle, whisk and bread hook.

Pots and Pans

Cast Iron Skillets – 6", 10" & 14", I love my well-seasoned cast iron skillets. Follow the manufacturer's instructions for seasoning and avoid using soap when washing unless you have to. Use hot water and sponge. I apply a little olive oil to the surface if the pan starts to look dry or rust.

Cast Iron Dutch Oven – 5 quart pot, which is perfect for stews, chili's, meats, etc.

Sauté pan, 16" – All Clad LTD® is my favorite brand.

2, 4 and 6 quart Pots with Lids – All Clad LTD® is my favorite brand.

Stock Pots - 2 gallon and 5 gallon, used for making stocks and big batches of soup.

Sheet Pans – half sheet pans or jelly roll pans. These are rimmed baking pans, usually 13" x 18", that fit into a standard oven.

Collections from an Aspen Chef
Favorite recipes with options to accommodate your dietary preferences

Pressure Cooker – The airtight seal around the lid traps steam and causes internal pressure to build, cooking food faster and locking in flavor.

Tools

Bamboo Steamer – a layered steamer used for cooking pork purses, dumplings, etc.

Chinois – a conical sieve with very fine mesh (you can also use a fine mesh strainer).

Cooling or Baking Racks – oven-safe racks made of metal, used for cooling or baking.

Graters – make sure to have a sharp grater that will do a fine grate and a regular grate. Also a nutmeg grater is good to have.

Knives – I have 7" Santoku and 10" Shun, both Japanese knives. A serrated knife for bread and tomatoes and a paring knife round out my collection. It's worth the money to buy good quality knifes. They will last you a lifetime.

Lemon Juicer – Sur la Table® has a great handheld lemon juicer I can't live without.

Melon Baller – an indispensable tool for scooping out fruit, cookie batter, pork purse filling. Sizes range from ⅜" to 1¼".

Metal Bowls – an assortment from small to large.

Parchment Paper – for baking.

Pastry Brushes – usually in the form of nylon or natural bristle.

Pepper Grinder – this is a personal choice, whatever feels good to you.

Potato Peeler – the simplest ones are the best. They just have to be sharp.

Strainers – one large, one medium and one small fine mesh strainer.

Thermometers: Candy, Meat and Oven Thermometers

Utensils - large spoons, ladles, tongs, kitchen scissors, measuring cups, measuring spoons and brushes. Spatulas - wooden, metal and rubber.

Zesters – I have a great hand tool from Italy that has 5 holes at the top for zesting citrus.

Collections from an Aspen Chef
Favorite recipes with options to accommodate your dietary preferences

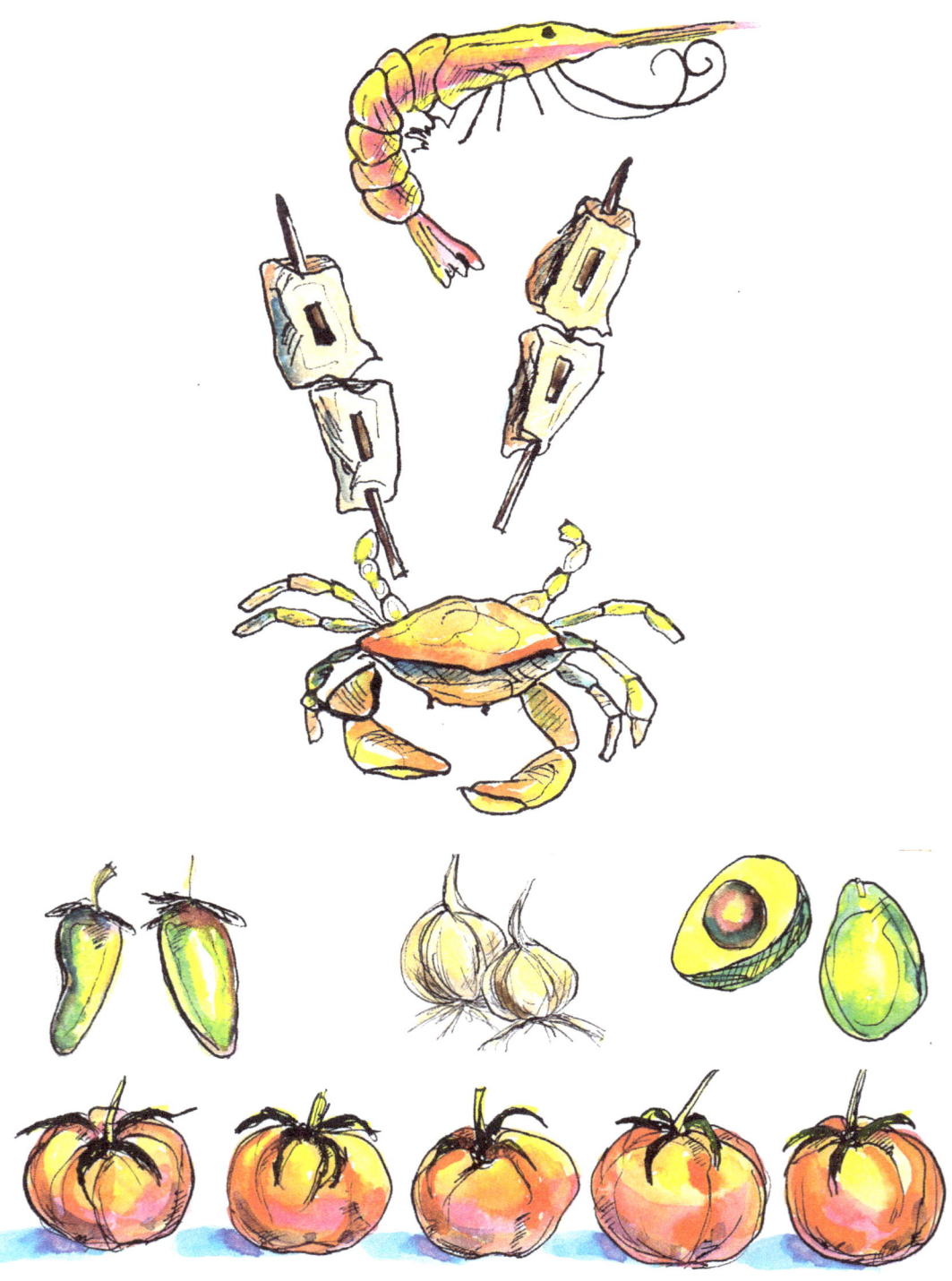

Collections from an Aspen Chef

Favorite recipes with options to accommodate your dietary preferences

Appetizers:

Lamb & Beef Satés w/Mint Sauce	18
Chicken Satés w/Thai Peanut Sauce	19
Southwestern Crab Cakes w/Spicy Chili Aioli	20
Southwestern Shrimp Ceviche	21
Jodie's Watermelon Wedges w/Tequila Sauce	22
Tequila Cured Salmon w/Pumpernickel Toast	23
Creole Grilled Shrimp w/Cajun Dipping Sauce	24
Kale Chips w/Lemon Juice & Olive Oil	25
Asparagus, Goat Cheese & Prosciutto Rolls	26
Duck & Shrimp Spring Rolls w/Nuoc Chom Sauce	27
Hoisin Turkey Spring Rolls	28
Pork Purses w/Ginger Soy Dipping Sauce	29
Honey, Lemon & Caper Grilled Shrimp	30
Crostini w/Fig Reduction, Brie & Bacon	31

GF = Gluten Free ~ DF = Dairy Free ~ VG = Vegan ~ ❄ = Freezes Well

Lamb or Beef Satés
With Mint Dipping Sauce

GF & DF

Serves 10 as an appetizer
3 lbs lamb or beef sirloin - large cubed, about 1 to 1½" pieces
Marinade
¼ C olive oil
¼ C fish sauce
6 limes - juiced
3 T tamari
2 T brown sugar
1 bunch cilantro - loosely chopped
2 stalks lemongrass - (can chop fine or slice big and remove before grilling)
1 (.66 oz) pkg of mint - loosely chopped
4 to 6 garlic cloves - peeled, finely chopped

Marinate cubed lamb or beef for 2 hours before grilling. Heat grill to medium high. Put one piece of meat on each skewer. Place on the grill to mark one side of the meat and flip putting a grill mark on other side. Cook until the center of meat is medium rare 125°, about 1-2 minutes per side. Serve with Mint dipping sauce.

Mint Sauce

GF, DF & VG

3 C fresh mint
1 clove garlic
2 tsp Dijon mustard
2 tsp honey
¼ C olive oil
¼ C rice wine vinegar
S & P

Add mint and garlic to a food processor. Pulse until fine chopped. Add honey, Dijon, vinegar, S & P. Pulse until mixed. Slowly drizzle olive oil through the top hole of your food processor and emulsify.

Chicken Satés
With Thai Peanut Sauce

GF & DF

Serves 10 as an appetizer

9 chicken breasts - 1" cubed (about 9 serving pieces per breast)

Marinade
½ C olive oil
1 C mirin
¼ C rice wine vinegar
¼ C brown sugar
1 T curry powder
2 to 4 T fresh ginger - peeled and finely grated
4 to 6 fresh garlic cloves - peeled and finely chopped

Marinate cubed chicken overnight. Put one or two pieces of cubed chicken on skewer. Line baking sheet with foil. Add skewers and bake at 350° for 10 minutes - flipping once. Or, grill on medium heat putting a grill mark on one side of the meat then flip to put a grill mark on other side. Cook about 3 minutes per side. Break one piece in half to check for doneness.

Tamari - is gluten free. Use in place of soy sauce.

Worcestershire® sauce - contains anchovies, it is not vegan! If you or a guest have fish allergies, omit it. Lee & Perrins® is GF.

Chinese Vinegar - does not contain fish, but may have gluten. Always read the label!

Peanut Sauce

❄ **GF, DF & VG**

2 T fresh ginger - peeled, coarsely chopped
2 cloves garlic - peeled
1 tsp Thai red curry paste (pg. 10)
½ C chunky peanut butter
¼ C tamari
3 ½ T sugar
3 ½ T Chinese black vinegar (or Worcestershire® sauce - not VG)
3 T sesame oil
5 T water

Place the garlic and ginger in a food processor and pulse until chopped. Add the rest of the ingredients and blend until smooth. Add more water to thin if needed.

This sauce freezes really well. You can make this 2 days ahead of time.

Vegan Option:
I prefer Thai Kitchen® red curry paste, it has no shellfish. Always check labels. Use Chinese black vinegar (VG).

In place of chicken, use sliced zucchini. Marinate ½ hr and grill long enough to put grill marks on both sides.

Or slice up carrots and jicima and serve cold with slightly warmed peanut sauce.

Southwestern Crab Cakes
With Spicy Chili Aioli Sauce

DF

Serves 10 as an appetizer

1 C fresh bread crumbs
1 stalk celery - fine dice
½ small white onion - fine dice
2 to 3 tsp olive oil
½ C mayonnaise
½ tsp dry mustard
¼ tsp garlic powder
¼ tsp onion powder
¼ tsp Tony Chachere's® Creole Seasoning
1 (16 oz) can lump or colossal blue crab meat
½ red pepper - small dice (optional)
½ poblano pepper or 2 jalapenos - small dice
2 tsp chopped cilantro - stemmed
1 egg white - whisk until frothy
3 to 4 T canola oil

> **Gluten Free Option:** To make this GF, you will need to omit the bread crumbs and make into a crab salad. Spread on rice crackers with the spicy aioli sauce on the side. I've tried substituting GF bread or crackers and it makes this dish mushy.

In a food processor, pulse fresh bread into small crumbs. Set aside. Sauté celery and onion in olive oil. Remove from heat and cool. Then mix with the remaining ingredients, including bread crumbs and form small crab cake patties. Sauté patties in canola oil until golden brown and crispy. Serve with spicy chile aioli sauce. You can sauté them ahead of time and reheat at 350°.

Spicy Chili Aioli Sauce   ❄ GF & DF

1 T olive oil
1 to 2 chipotle peppers - canned in adobo sauce
1 red pepper - large chop
1 poblano pepper - large chop
3 garlic cloves - peeled
½ white onion - large chop
4 green onions - large chop
½ bunch cilantro - stemmed

Sauté the above ingredients in olive oil. Remove from heat and cool. Transfer to a food processor and pulse to a coarse chop. Divide your chopped ingredients into ¼ C portions. Freeze all, but one of your ¼ C portions. This freezes well for up to 6 months.

To Finish Sauce: add one ¼ C portion of Spicy Chile Aiole Sauce to:
¼ C mayonnaise
2 tsp balsamic vinegar, 1 tsp cumin, ½ tsp dry mustard, S & P
Mix well and serve with crab cakes.

Kale Chips
With Lemon Juice & Olive Oil

GF, DF & VG

Serves 6 as an appetizer
2 bunches curly kale
2 lemons - juiced
4 T olive oil
pinch of fine sea salt
pinch of cayene (optional)

Preheat oven to 300°. Line a baking sheet with parchment.

Wash the kale and remove stems. Tear into large pieces, approximately 4 pieces per leaf (they will shrink with baking). Place in a bowl and add salt, lemon juice and olive oil. Toss until well coated.

Place on a baking sheet and bake for 20-25 minutes, turning every 5 minutes or so. Bake until leaves are crispy, not burnt.

I've found that a convection oven will not get the same results as a regular oven. Convection seems to take longer and tends to burn the kale.

Asparagus & Goat Cheese
Rolled in Prosciutto & Baked

GF

I had this at a dinner party 20 years ago, this is my rendition.

Serves 10 as an appetizer

2 bunches asparagus
1 (4 to 5 oz) log goat cheese - plain (you won't use it all)
10-15 slices prosciutto

Cut off asparagus ends and blanch (see side-bar). Run under cold water and set aside to cool. Slice each prosciutto piece into 4 pieces approximately 1" wide by 3" long. Smear ½ tsp dab of goat cheese on the prosciutto, lay asparagus on top, like a cross, and roll the prosciutto around the asparagus. (As if the asparagus has a belly scarf.)

> **To Blanch -**
> Drop your veggie into boiling water for a short period of time, about one minute. (With asparagus, I leave in boiling water just until it turns bright green.) Strain and run under cold water.

Bake at 350° for 10 minute until hot. Serve immediately or at room temp.

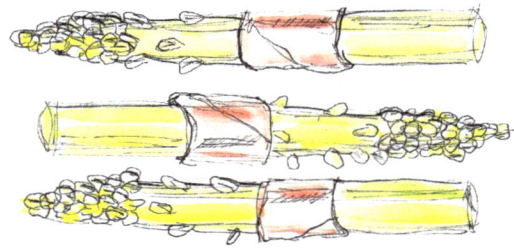

Duck & Shrimp Spring Rolls
With Nuoc Cham Dipping Sauce

GF & DF

Serves 10 as an appetizer

Nuoc Cham Sauce
4 T water
4 tsp sugar
¼ tsp crushed red pepper
4 serrano chilies - sliced
4 cloves garlic - minced
4 lemons - juiced
4 T rice wine vinegar
¾ C fish sauce

Bring water and sugar to boil. Immediately turn off and cool. Add the rest of the ingredients to the simple sugar mix. This can be made 2 days ahead of time.

Spring Rolls
1 pkg round rice paper sheets for spring rolls (if possible, use the ones with the rose label)

Assemble - Have Ready in Side Dishes
1 lb shrimp - peeled, deveined and cooked, sliced in ½ lengthwise
1 smoked duck breast - julienne sliced or shredded
1 red pepper - julienne sliced
1 bunch green onion - julienne sliced
3 carrots - blanched and julienne sliced
1 cucumber - seeded and julienne sliced
1 bunch cilantro - stemmed and chopped
1 (.66 oz pkg) mint - stemmed and chopped
1 (.66 oz pkg) basil - chiffonade
2 heads Bibb lettuce - torn into 2 inch pieces, remove ribs

> **Vegan Option:**
> To make this VG, eliminate the shrimp and duck. Replace with cooked cellophane noodles to take the place of the meat. Boil noodles al dente, strain and hold in cold water until needed. Serve with Peanut Sauce pg. 19.

My friend Ike, who grew up in Hawaii, told me a trick he learned from his Japanese mother. Fill a large plate with lukewarm water and soak one rice paper sheet at a time. When it gets pliable but not too soft, take it out and place on a moistened wood cutting board. Spread it out with your fingers, (add your layers to the bottom third of your paper). First add Bibb lettuce and 3 slices each of shrimp and duck. Then add a little of each of the remaining ingredients. Fold in the sides, then roll from the bottom up. Roll it as tight as you can. Store under a moist paper towel until ready to use. These will hold for at least 3 hours.

Experiment with at least 2 brands of rice papers to see how they hold up. The fresher the better.

Collections from an Aspen Chef ~ Cindy Rogers

Hoisin Turkey Spring Rolls
Wrapped in Bibb Lettuce

GF & DF

Serves 10-15 as an appetizer

1½ lbs ground turkey
½ C hoisin sauce (check the label for GF)
1 (8oz) can sliced water chestnuts - chopped
3 green onions - chopped
2 T basil - chiffonade
2 T mint - stemmed and minced
S & P
2 heads Bibb lettuce - remove ribs
1 pkg round rice paper sheets for spring rolls (if possible, use the ones with the rose label)

Cook turkey in a skillet until brown. Add S & P to taste. Add hoisin, waterchestnuts and green onions. Mix well. This can be made a day or two ahead of time.

One hour before assembling, add the basil and mint. Stir well.

Assemble

Fill a large plate with lukewarm water and soak one rice paper sheet at a time. When it gets pliable but not too soft, take it out and place on a moistened wood cutting board. Spread it out with your fingers, (add your layers to the bottom third of your paper). Place a piece of bibb lettuce on the bottom end of the rice paper and add your hoisin meat filling (about ¼ C). Fold in the sides then roll from the bottom up. Roll it as tight as you can.

These can hold under a moist paper towel for 2-3 hours.

Cut into 3 pieces and serve.

Pork Purses

With Ginger Soy Dipping Sauce & Mustard Sauce

DF

Serves 10-15 as an appetizer

1 lb ground pork - (Whole Foods has good DF ground pork)
¼ lb prosciutto - sliced and chopped
½ C bok choy – leaves and stalks, chopped
1 (8 oz) can sliced water chestnuts - chopped
1 T tamari
2 tsp rice wine vinegar
3 T green onions - chopped
3 T basil - chiffonade
3 T mint - chopped
1½" fresh ginger - peel and fine grate
1 tsp sesame oil
1 egg - beaten
1 tsp brown sugar
1 pkg small square wonton wrappers for purses
Pam® spray
bamboo steamer - 4 tiers (buy at Asian store)

Gluten Free Option: Use cabbage leaves on the bottom of the steamers and steam the pork balls without the wonton wrappers. Serve with toothpicks and dipping sauces.

Mix all the above ingredients, except wonton wrappers. Take wonton wrappers and lay out on cutting board. Add about a 1" ball of pork mix to the center of wrapper. Grasp all four sides, pull up and turn around pork ball to make an open purse.

Put an empty bamboo steamer in a 14" sauce pan. Add water, about 2" up the side of the empty steamer. Bring to a boil. Spray Pam® on the bottom of the next bamboo steamer and add purses. (I can fit 11 purses into a 12" steamer without touching.) Add more bamboo steamer layers as needed. Steam the purses over boiling water for 25 minutes. Make sure the water doesn't evaporate out of the sauce pan.

Ginger Soy Dipping Sauce

GF, DF & VG

4 T Tamari (GF alternative to soy sauce)
3 T rice wine vinegar
2 tsp canola oil
1 tsp sesame oil
1 tsp each of: minced garlic, fine grated ginger and chopped green onions
2 T brown sugar

Whisk all the ingredients in a bowl. Whisk again before serving.

Mustard Sauce

GF, DF & VG

Take equal amounts of Colemans® dry mustard and water and whisk untill mixed. Serve with Pork Purses and Ginger Soy Dipping Sauce.

Collections from an Aspen Chef ~ Cindy Rogers

Honey, Lemon, Caper Grilled Shrimp
With a Sweet & Savory Reduction Sauce

Serves 10 as an appetizer   **GF & DF**

1 lb large shrimp - peeled and deveined, tails on
3 T capers (plus 1 T for garnish)
2 T pickling liquid from capers
½ C honey
2 tsp dry sherry
1 lemon - zest
1 lemon - juiced
¼ C Limoncello
2 tsp kosher salt
1½ C extra virgin olive oil

> **Limoncello -**
> Limoncello is my favorite Italian liqueur, made from lemons. When I was on the Almafi coast and Cinque Terre, I found some amazing local vendors.

Garnish
1 T capers for garnish
2 lemons - cut into wedges

Place shrimp in bowl or Ziploc bag. Puree the rest of the ingredients in a food processor. Add to the shrimp and marinate for 1-4 hours. Save the marinade. Grill shrimp over medium heat, about 3 minutes per side or until done. In a sauce pan, on medium heat, reduce the reserved marinade to a thick syrup and toss over grilled shrimp just before serving. Garnish with the remaining 1 T capers. Arrange the lemon wedges around the edges.

Serve with toothpicks and bowls to catch the tails.

It's very important to remember if you reserve your marinade to always cook and reduce down. (The raw meat in the marinade will make you very sick.)

Fig Crostini with Brie & Bacon
With a Port Wine Fig Reduction Sauce & Caramelized Onions

Serves 10 as an appetizer

1 baguette - thinly slice
3 T olive oil
5 T butter
2 bags Mission or golden figs - quartered and stemmed
2 C port - or enough to cover figs
4 T fig jam
½ C sugar
few drops of balsamic vinegar
2 onions - sliced in thin rounds and quartered
8 pieces of bacon - cooked and torn into small pieces
1 wedge of goat Brie - softened to room temperature

Gluten Free Option: Use a gluten free baguette for your crostini. You can find gluten free baguettes, brands like Udi's® or Against the Grain®, in the freezer section of your grocery store.

Crostini Melt 2 T butter and 2 T olive oil. Thinly slice a baguette, place on parchment lined baking sheet. With a pastry brush, lightly brush slices with olive oil/butter mix. Bake at 350° for 5-10 minutes, or until golden brown.

Fig Reduction Sauce
Add figs to a sauce pan and add enough port wine to cover the figs (about 2 C). Add the fig jam, ¼ C sugar and a few drops of balsamic vinegar. Heat all the ingredients and simmer until syrupy. Set aside.

Caramelized Onions Add onions, ¼ C sugar, 1 tsp salt, 3 T butter and 1 T olive oil. Sauté on medium low until the onions turn a caramel brown (half hour to 1 hour). Set aside.

Assemble Lay out crostini. Add a smear of goat Brie, then add 2 fig quarters coated in reduction sauce, a few caramelized onions and a torn piece of bacon - platter and serve.

If you have any fig reduction sauce with quartered figs left over this is a good recipe to use.

Figs Rolled in Prosciutto with Goat Cheese or Roquefort - *Serves 10*   **GF**

fig reduction sauce above w/quartered figs
½ pound sliced prosciutto
1 (4 to 5 oz) log of goat cheese or 1 (5 oz) pkg of Society Blue Roquefort

Lay out a prosciutto piece and slice into 4 segments. Add a dab of cheese and a fig quarter coated in reduction sauce. Roll the fig and cheese up in the prosciutto and hold with a toothpick. Bake at 350° for 5 minutes. Can serve warm or at room temperature.

Collections from an Aspen Chef
Favorite recipes with options to accommodate your dietary preferences

Collections from an Aspen Chef
Favorite recipes with options to accommodate your dietary preferences

Salads:

Kale & Brussel Sprouts Salad w/Beets	34
Niçoise Salad w/Seared Ahi	35
German Potato Salads - Classic & Harald's	36
Chicken Milanese	37
Moroccan Chicken Salad	38
Vietnamese Chicken & Shrimp Salad	39
Lee's Arugula, Watercress Salad	40
Bonnie's Inspired Endive Salad	41
Cindy's Caesar (Eggless)	42
Pomegranate Vinaigrette, Danish Blue Cheese & Cindy's Honey Dijon Vinaigrette	43
Orange Dijon Vinaigrette, Yellow Miso & Bragg Vinaigrette & Laura's Dressing	44
Lemon Dijon Vinaigrette, Fig Balsamic Dressing & Raspberry Basil Vinaigrette	45

GF = Gluten Free ～ DF = Dairy Free ～ VG = Vegan ～ ❄ = Freezes Well

Kale & Brussels Sprouts Salad
With Fuji Apples, Marinated Beets & Cashew Lemon Vinaigrette

GF, DF & VG

This is a great salad to make ahead of time, hours before your guests arrive.
Serves 12

2 bunches kale - chiffonade
10 to 15 Brussels sprouts- remove outer leaves and thinly slice
2 Fuji or Honeycrisp apples - julienne
1 (6 oz) bag dried apricots - fine dice
½ C cashews, raw - large chop

> **Chiffonade -**
> Wash kale, remove and discard the spine before you chiffonade. Lay leaves flat on top of each other, roll up and thinly slice across the roll with a very sharp knife.

In a big bowl combine the kale, brussels sprouts, apples and apricots. Coat with Cashew Lemon Vinaigrette (below) and toss. This should be done at least 3-6 hours before you serve the salad so the kale can absorb the vinaigrette. Add beets (below) just prior to serving salad, otherwise they will color the salad red. Top with chopped cashews.

Optional - You can add shaved Parmesan cheese or Manchego cheese on top for garnish. I like to use a potato peeler to shave cheese.

Cashew Lemon Vinaigrette
2-3 lemons - juiced
1 tsp Dijon
½ C raw cashews
½ C extra virgin olive oil
S & P

Add ingredients to a food processor and pulse until cashews are chopped into small bits (not a paste). If the vinaigrette is too thick, add more lemon juice and olive oil.

Marinated Beets
3 red beets
1 C balsamic vinegar - enough to cover beets

Wash dirt off beets, leave skin on and trim off the top and tail of the beet. Cover with water and boil for 45 minutes to 1 hour - until fork tender.

Run the beets under cold water and rub the skin off.

Then either slice or cube beets and put into a container. Cover and marinate in balsamic vinegar at least 1 hour. Leftovers will hold in the refrigerator for 1 week.

Niçoise Salad with Seared Ahi

GF & DF

With Black Olive Tapenade & Lemon Vinaigrette

Serves 12

1 lb golden fingerling potatoes - boiled, cooled and ¼" sliced
3 C green beans - boiled until tender (about 5 minutes)
1 C Niçoise olives - with or without pits (warn your guest if they have pits)
1 small container of cherry tomatoes - washed and halved
1 (3.5 oz) jar capers
½ C Kalamata olives - pitted
6 boiled eggs - peeled and quartered
4 heads Bibb lettuce - cleaned and carefully torn, don't bruise

3 (7 oz) pieces of sushi grade Ahi
    Marinate for 1–2 hours in:
    ½ C black olive tapenade (below)
    ¼ C tamari

Pan sear or grill for 2 minutes for rare and 6 minutes for medium rare. Slice before serving.

Black Olive Tapenade

1 T olive oil
3 cloves garlic - peeled
5 anchovy fillets
2 T capers
1½ C Kalamata olives - pitted
¼ tsp fresh cracked black pepper

Place all the ingredients in a food processor and pulse untill finely chopped.

Black Olive Tapenade Salad Dressing

½ C Black Olive Tapenade
¼ C mayonnaise
Mix well.

Lemon Dijon Vinaigrette

GF, DF & VG

2 lemons - juiced
2 T rice wine vinegar
4 tsp Dijon mustard
½ C extra virgin olive oil
S & P

Whisk until emulsified or pulse in a food processor to emulsify.

Assemble- First layer - toss Bibb lettuce, green beans, tomatoes and olives in the lemon vinaigrette, place on platter. Second layer- toss the potatoes in black olive tapenade salad dressing and add to platter. To finish, add the capers, eggs and seared sliced Ahi.

German Potato Salad-Classic & Harald's
One Hot, One Cold...Both Delicious

My Classic German potato salad is a combination of three wonderful lady's who all had roots in Germany. On a trip to Bremen, Germany, to visit my friend Harald, he made me his version of a cold German potato salad.

Classic Hot German Potato Salad - *Serves 15*   GF & DF
5 lbs red potatoes, with skin - boil until fork tender, not mushy - large dice
½ bunch celery - small dice
½ tsp celery seeds
6 hard boiled eggs - sliced (I like to use an egg slicer)
1 lb bacon - cooked and broken into ½" pieces, reserve ¼ C bacon grease
1 onion - small dice
¼ C sugar
½ C cider vinegar
½ C cold water and 2 T GF cornstarch (mix w/fork)
S & P

Add potatoes, celery and celery seeds to a large bowl. Set aside. Sauté onion until translucent in ¼ C reserved bacon grease. Add sugar, cider vinegar, cold water/cornstarch mix and stir until thickened. Toss over potatoes and celery and mix until combined. Top with eggs and bacon. Serve warm or at room temperature.

Harald's Cold Potato Salad - *Serves 10*   GF & DF
2 lbs fingerling potatoes, with skin - boil until fork tender, large dice
½ bunch celery - small dice
1 Fuji apple - small dice
6 sweet pickles (or Bread & Butter Pickles pg 96) - small dice
1 T pickle juice
½ C green olives - sliced or halved
½ C mayonnaise
1 T Dijon mustard
S & P

Mix and refrigerate for an hour or so. Serve cold or at room temperature.

Vegan Option: Use Vegenaise® in place of mayonnaise. You can find this at your local health food store. It's hard to tell the difference.

Chicken Milanese Salad
With Arugula, Tomatoes & Shaved Parmesan Cheese

Serves 4

4 veal chops or 4 chicken breasts
3 eggs
1 C flour
1 C bread crumbs
1 C parmesan cheese: ½ C finely grate and ½ C shaved with potato peeler
3 to 5 T olive oil for cooking
1 bag of arugula (about 4 C)
1 small container of cherry tomatoes - halved
½ C pine nuts - toasted (pg 73)
1 lemon - cut into wedges

For the veal: partly separate the meat from the bone of 4 veal rib chops. Individually place chops between sheets of plastic wrap to keep the mess down when pounding. Working away from the center, use a skillet or pounder to flatten to ¼" thick. If using chicken breast, put into a Ziploc® bag and pound to ¼" thick. Preheat oven to 300°. You will need three bowls: place flour in one, slightly beat eggs in another and mix ½ cup bread crumbs and ½ cup finely grated parmesan cheese in the third bowl. Dredge each chop or breast in flour, then egg, then bread crumb/parmesan mix, pressing the coating onto the meat.

Heat 2 to 3 T olive oil in skillet over medium high heat. Sauté each chop until browned, about 3-4 minutes. Reduce heat to medium, flip chops or breasts and cook 5-6 minutes longer. Transfer the chops or breasts to a baking sheet and keep them warm in the oven while you cook the remaining meat and prepare your salad. Lightly dress salad of arugula and tomatoes with a Balsamic Dressing and sprinkle with pine nuts and shaved parmesan. Top salad with cooked veal chop or sliced chicken. Serve with lemon wedges on the side.

Balsamic Dressing   GF, DF & VG

⅓ C balsamic vinegar
1 tsp Dijon mustard
¼ C olive oil
S & P

Whisk to emulsify.

Moroccan Chicken Salad
With Chermoula Sauce, a.k.a. Lee's Cha Cha Sauce

GF & DF

While visiting friends Lee and Jules on the big island of Hawaii, I had fun modifying this chermoula sauce with all the amazing citrus and herbs they had growing on their property. This sauce became one of Lee's favorites and is now known as Lee's Cha Cha Sauce in Hawi, HI.

Serves 8

6 chicken breasts - pounded to ¼" thick

Reserve ½ C Chermoula Sauce for garnish. Marinate chicken in remaining Chermoula Sauce, for about 2 hours. Grill 5 minutes per side. Transfer to a plate, cover with foil and allow to cool to room temperature.

Chermoula Sauce, a.k.a. Lee's Cha Cha Sauce

GF, DF & VG

1 bunch of cilantro - stemmed
1 bunch parsley - stemmed
1 (.66 oz) pkg oregano - stemmed - optional
1 (.66 oz) pkg mint - stemmed - optional
2 cloves garlic - peeled
1 to 2 jalapenos - stemmed and seeded
2 lemons - juiced
2 limes - juiced
1 orange - juiced (or 1 T frozen OJ concentrate)
2 tsp ground cumin
1 T paprika
¼ tsp cayenne pepper
1 C extra virgin olive oil
S & P

Add the cilantro, parsley, oregano, mint, garlic and jalapenos to a food processor and pulse until finely chopped. Add lemon, lime and orange juice, cumin, paprika, cayenne pepper. Slowly drizzle in the olive oil until incorporated. S & P to taste. This will hold in the refrigerator for a week.

Salad

GF, DF & VG

2 bags of spring green mix
2 heads of Bibb lettuce
1 box cherry tomatoes - sliced in half

Simple Vinaigrette

GF, DF & VG

1 tsp Dijon mustard
1 tsp honey
¼ C rice wine vinegar
½ C olive oil
S & P to taste

Pulse in a food processor until emulsified.

Assemble - Toss greens with vinaigrette to taste. Slice grilled chicken on the diagonal. Add on top of greens. Top chicken with reserved chermoula sauce.

Vietnamese Chicken-Shrimp Salad
With Nuoc Cham Sauce and Thai Peanut Sauce
Serves 15

Nuoc Cham Sauce - *(Vietnamese dipping sauce)*   **GF & DF**
4 T water
4 tsp sugar
¼ tsp crushed red pepper
4 serrano chilis - sliced into rounds
4 cloves garlic - minced
4 lemons - juiced
4 T rice wine vinegar
¾ C fish sauce

Bring water and sugar to boil. Immediately turn off and cool. Add the rest of the ingredients. Put into a container. This will hold in the refrigerator for a week.

Peanut Sauce   ❄ **GF, DF & VG**
1 T fresh ginger - peeled and ½" cube
3 cloves garlic - peeled
1 tsp Thai red curry paste (pg. 10)
½ C chunky peanut butter
¼ C tamari (gluten free soy sauce)
3½ T sugar
3½ T Chinese black vinegar (or Worcestershire® sauce - not VG)
3 T sesame oil
5 T water

> **Fish Allergies -** Worcestershire® sauce has anchovies. Check label for GF (pg. 11). Omit and replace with tamari if you need to.

Puree ginger and garlic in food processor. Add the rest of the ingredients and add more water if the sauce needs thinning. This freezes well.

Pad Thai Rice Noodles - 1 pkg. Cook al denté, strain and hold in cold water, until needed.

Chicken Marinade   **GF & DF**
6 to 8 chicken breasts or 8 to 10 thighs - skinless, boneless.
½ C rice wine vinegar
½ C mirin
2 T fresh ginger - peeled and minced
4 cloves garlic - peeled and minced
¼ C tamari
4 T brown sugar
¾ C olive oil or canola oil

Mix all ingredients and marinate chicken overnight. Grill about 5 minutes per side. Slice.

Shrimp - 2 lbs large shrimp - peeled and deveined. Toss in olive oil and cajun seasoning. Grill for 3-5 minutes per side.

Assemble - Put rice noodles in center of platter. Then around noodles, layer 2 heads Bibb lettuce - torn, half head sliced red cabbage, 2 seeded sliced cucumbers, 1 sliced red and yellow pepper, 1 package bean sprouts, 3 julienne sliced blanched carrots, 1 bunch sliced green onions, cashews, 1 package each, mint and basil, and 1 bunch cilantro - chopped. Top with sliced chicken and shrimp, serve with Nuoc Chom Sauce and Peanut sauce on the side.

Lee's Arugula, Watercress Salad
With Fuji Apples, Fennel, Endive and Caramelized Pecans

GF, DF & VG

Lee has been a long time client and friend. She and I came up with this salad a few years ago and it's been a favorite ever since.

Serves 8

2 bunchs watercress
2 bags arugula
2 fennel bulbs - shave with potato peeler
2 Fuji apples - julienne
3 Belgian endive - slice into half moons
4 lemons - juiced
goat cheese - crumbled (optional not VG)
caramelized pecans

Clean and trim watercress. Clean arugula. Set aside. In a bowl, add fennel, endive and apples and soak in lemon juice to keep from browning. Just before serving, drain and add to the arugula and watercress. Toss with vinaigrette, then top with Caramelized Pecans and goat cheese.

Caramelized Pecans

2 C pecans - raw, whole (peanut oil free, check label)
4 C boiling water
⅔ C powdered sugar
1 tsp kosher salt
2 pinches cayenne
2 pinches chile powder

Drop nuts into boiling water and boil 30 seconds, drain. Toss nuts in powdered sugar, salt and spices. Bake at 350° on foil-lined sheet pan until golden brown, about 10-20 minutes. Keep checking the nuts so they don't burn.

Honey Dijon Vinaigrette

2 tsp honey
3 tsp Dijon mustard
⅓ C rice wine vinegar
½ C olive oil
S & P

Pulse in a food processor until emulsified. Leftover vinaigrette will hold in the refrigerator for at least a month.

Bonnie's Inspired Endive Salad
With Cherry Port Vinaigrette & Caramelized Walnuts

GF

Bonnie was my dear friend who loved to spoil her friends and family with wonderful meals. This is my version of a salad I had at her house for dinner one evening.

Cherry Port Vinaigrette - *Serves 8*   **GF, DF & VG**

⅔ C port
1 T shallot - finely chopped
¼ C red wine vinegar
2 T sugar
½ C olive oil
½ C dried cherries

> **Vegan and Dairy Free Option:**
> To make this VG & DF, eliminate the Roquefort.
>
> For VG walnuts, use Caramelized Pecan Recipe, pg 40.

Cook first 4 ingredients until alcohol is evaporated - about 1 minute. Cool and whisk in oil. Add cherries. You will need to whisk or shake vigorously before tossing on salad.

Caramelized Walnuts   **GF & DF**

2 C walnuts - raw, whole (peanut oil free, check label)
2 egg whites
3 T sugar
3 T kosher salt

Mix all the ingredients. Bake at 350° on foil-lined sheet pan until golden brown about 10-20 minutes. Keep checking the nuts so they don't burn.

Salad   **GF**

1 head frisse or curly endive
2 heads Belgian endive
1 bag baby spring greens
1 pkg Society Blue Roquefort
2 pears or Fuji apples

Wash curly endive or frisse and spring greens. Tear into bite size pieces, place in a bowl and set aside. Slice Belgian endive on the rounds, slice pears or apples into thin wedges (you can toss Belgian endive and pears in lemon juice to keep from browning). Break up Roquefort cheese. Toss with Cherry Port Vinaigrette and top with Caramelized Walnuts. Set aside some fruit, Roquefort and caramelized walnuts to garnish the salad.

Cindy's Caesar Salad (Eggless)
With Parmesan Chips and Homemade Croutons

Caesar Salad Dressing - *Serves 8*
2 cloves garlic - peeled
1 (5 oz) can of rolled anchovies with capers or 6 anchovies in oil
3 tsp Dijon mustard
2 lemons - juiced
¾ C Parmigiano Reggiano cheese - finely grated
¾ to 1 C olive oil
S & P

Add garlic and anchovies to a food processor and pulse till minced. Add Dijon and lemon juice. Drizzle in the olive oil until emulsified. Add grated parmesan cheese, S & P to taste. Sometimes the lemons are strong, so add more cheese and olive oil to adjust flavor.

Parmesan Chips
1 large chunk of Parmigiano Reggiano cheese

Finely grate Parmigiano Reggiano, add ¼ inch high layer to a parchment lined sheet pan. Bake at 350° for 10-20 minutes until golden brown.
Take out of the oven, pat the grease off with a paper towel and flip onto another piece of parchment paper. Peel parchment off Parmigiano Reggaino and pat the under side as well. Break into pieces when cool.

Croutons
1 French bread loaf - cut into 1" cubes
3 T melted butter and 3 T olive oil
Italian herbs
S & P

Toss cubed French bread in equal mixture of melted butter and olive oil. Sprinkle with seasoning. Bake at 400° for 10 –15 minutes until golden brown.

Salad -
3 heads of romaine lettuce
Wash and discard brown edges. Slice into ¾ to 1" inch slices. Place in ice cold water to chill. Drain and dry in salad spinner.

Assemble -
Put chilled romaine lettuce into a big bowl and toss with dressing. Add parmesan chips and croutons.

Gluten Free Option: To make this GF, delete the croutons, it's delicious without. Just use the Parmesan Chips.

Cow Dairy Free Option: I use a really hard goat cheese in place of parmesan in the dressing, and omit the chips.

Parmigiano Reggiano- Seems to be the only cheese that works with these chips.

Salad Dressings...
Pomegranate, Danish Blue cheese & Honey Dijon Vinaigrette

Pomegranate Vinaigrette GF, DF & VG
¼ C pomegranate molasses
2 tsp honey
3 tsp Dijon mustard
¼ C rice wine vinegar
½ C olive oil
S & P

Pulse in a food processor or whisk until emulsified.

Danish Blue Cheese Dressing GF
½ C Stella blue cheese or Society Blue Roquefort
2 T mayonnaise
3 T buttermilk
2 T yogurt
2 tsp white wine vinegar
¼ tsp sugar
¼ tsp garlic powder
S & P

Whisk until combined. While mixing you may want to break up the blue cheese or Roquefort with a fork.

Honey Dijon Vinaigrette GF, DF & VG
2 tsp honey
3 tsp Dijon mustard
⅓ C rice wine vinegar
½ C olive oil
S & P

Pulse in a food processor or whisk until emulsified.

Salad Dressings...
Orange Dijon Vinaigrette, Miso/Bragg & Laura's Dressing

Orange Dijon Vinaigrette.   GF, DF & VG
⅓ C frozen orange juice concentrate
¼ C red wine vinegar
2 tsp Dijon mustard
2 T scallions - chopped
1 C extra virgin olive oil
S & P

Whisk or pulse in a food processor until emulsified.

Yellow Miso & Bragg Vinaigrette   GF, DF & VG
¼ C yellow or white miso
¼ C Bragg Liquid Aminos (GF alternative to soy sauce) has soy
1 clove garlic - minced
½ C rice wine vinegar
pinch red pepper flakes

Whisk or pulse in a food processor until emulsified.

Laura's Dressing   DF & VG
2 T Dijon mustard
2 cloves garlic - minced
¼ C mirin
2 T soy sauce (use tamari for GF)
½ C rice wine vinegar
½ C olive oil
S & P

Whisk or put all the ingredients in a jar and shake vigorously until combined.

Salad Dressings...
Lemon Dijon Vinaigrette, Balsamic & Raspberrry Basil Vinaigrette

Lemon Dijon Vinaigrette   GF, DF & VG
2 lemons - juiced
3 tsp Dijon mustard
½ C extra virgin olive oil (add more if too lemony)
S & P

Whisk in a bowl or pulse in a food processor until emulsified.

Fig Balsamic Dressing   GF, DF & VG
¼ C fig balsamic vinegar
2 tsp Dijon mustard
¼ tsp kosher salt
⅛ tsp fresh cracked pepper
1 tsp sugar
¾ C extra virgin olive oil

Whisk in a bowl until combined.

Raspberry Basil Vinaigrette   GF, DF & VG
1 bag frozen raspberries
1 (.66 oz) pkg of basil - stemmed
1 T Dijon mustard
2 T honey
½ C rice wine vinegar
1 C extra virgin olive oil
¼ tsp kosher salt

Thaw frozen raspberries. Pulse in a food processor until pureed, then strain the seeds out in a chinois, (a conical sieve with very fine mesh). Clean the food processor to remove any seeds and add the strained raspberries and the remaining ingredients. Pulse until emulsified.

Collections from an Aspen Chef
Favorite recipes with options to accommodate your dietary preferences

GF = Gluten Free ~ DF = Dairy Free ~ VG = Vegan ~ ❄ = Freezes Well

Collections from an Aspen Chef
Favorite recipes with options to accommodate your dietary preferences

Soups:

Fall Kabocha Squash Soup	48
Beef Bourguignon	49
Dad's Beef Chili	50
Green Chili & Pork Tenderloin Soup	51
Chicken & Red Chili Posole	52
Cindy's Homemade Chicken Stock w/Dumplings	53
Di Baby's Vegan Chili	54
Filé Gumbo	55
Caramelized Onion Soup w/Gruyere Crostini	56
Carrot Ginger Soup w/Candied Cashews	57
Ribollita Soup	58
Potato Leek Soup	59
Vegan Lentil Soup	60
French Sorrel Soup	61
Chunky Gazpacho	62
Split Pea Soup	63

Fall Kabocha Squash Soup
With Chicken or Vegetarian Stock

❄ GF & DF

Kabocha squash is a wonderful fall treat, it has a sweet savory flavor. It's the squash that shows up in the fall with the butternut squash, the one that looks like a green striped contorted pumpkin.

Serves 12

2 to 3 T olive oil
4 leeks - white and light green parts only, cleaned, ¼" thinly slice
8 stalks celery - medium dice
1 kabocha squash - seeded, peeled and medium dice
½ head cauliflower - cut into little florets
8 C chicken stock or vegetable stock
1 (28 oz) can diced tomatoes
1 T fresh marjoram or 3 tsp dried marjoram
¼ tsp white pepper
1 (15 oz) can cannellini beans - rinsed and strained
1 bunch Swiss chard - stemmed, chiffonade
S & P

Place olive oil, leeks and celery into a 2 gallon stock pot, sauté 8 minutes. Add Kabocha squash, cauliflower, chicken or vegetable stock, tomatoes, marjoram and white pepper. Cook on a low rolling boil until veggies are tender, about 40 minutes. Add beans and Swiss chard and cook 5 minutes longer.
Add S & P to taste.

This soup freezes well.

Vegan Option:
I prefer Better Than Bouillion®, either no-chicken base or vegetable base instead of chicken stock.

Cleaning Leeks -
Cut off root end. Cut green off 1 to 2" above white. I usually have a 5" segment left. Cut the trimmed leek in half lengthwise and run under cold water until the dirt is removed. Check in between layers to see that all the dirt is gone.

Beef Bourguignon
With Grassfed Beef

❄ DF

Serves 12

3 to 5 T canola oil
5 lbs stew beef (chuck or sirloin cuts)
½ C flour
1 (750 ml) bottle burgundy wine
2 T olive oil
2 yellow onions - medium dice
8 carrots - peeled, thick diagonal slices
3 cloves garlic- minced
½ bunch fresh parsley - coarsely chopped
6 red or Yukon Gold potatoes - large 1" dice or 1lb bag of fingerling potatoes cut in half
2 tsp tomato paste
2 bay leaves
1 (.66 oz) pkg fresh thyme - chopped or 1½ tsp dry thyme
chicken or beef stock, enough to cover meat and vegetables
2 bags frozen pearl onions
1 bag frozen peas - thawed (add at the end)
S & P
sour cream - optional (not DF)

> **Gluten Free Option:**
> Sauté the meat in oil and eliminiate the flour dredge. Add 2 T arrowroot to ½ C chicken stock. Whisk into the soup the last 15 minutes of cooking.

> **Deglazing -**
> A cooking technique using liquid to remove and dissolve browned food residue from the bottom of a pan. The browned bits are called *fond* (french for "base" or "foundation"); and is used to create delicious sauces, soups and gravies.

Cut stew beef into 1" cubes. Dredge meat in flour. Brown meat in batches in canola oil, leaving about ½" space between meat pieces. Deglaze pan with wine after each batch. Set aside in a bowl. Repeat until all the meat is cooked, adding more canola oil for sauté as needed.

Place olive oil, onions and carrots into a Dutch oven or 2 gallon oven safe stock pot, sauté 8 minutes. Add the sautéd meat and the rest of the ingredients (except frozen peas). Cover all the ingredients with chicken or beef stock (about 6–8 C). Cook in a 350° oven with the lid on for about 3 hours. Stir every half hour or so.

Add thawed peas at the very end before serving. (The peas will get mushy if you add them too early). Add S & P to taste.

Garnish with sour cream - optional.

Dad's Beef Chili
With Grassfed Beef and Pinto Beans

❄ **GF & DF**

My dad likes his chili super hot, if you use chile piquins and habeneros, use caution. Dad would add leftover chunks of cooked beef along with the ground beef and pork. This is my tamed down version.

Serves 12

4 lbs grassfed ground beef or 4 lbs ground elk
2 lbs Italian sausage (GF & DF, check labels)
1 (12 oz) bottle gluten free lager (or stout beer - not GF)
3 to 4 T olive oil
1 large or 2 medium onions - small dice
1 bunch celery – small dice
1 yellow pepper - small dice
4 carrots peeled - fine dice (or chop in the food processor)
2 T chili powder
5 (28 oz) cans diced tomatoes
3 (28 oz) cans tomato sauce
4 cloves garlic - minced
4 jalapenos - fine dice
1 C roasted green chiles (½ C if they are spicy hot) - small dice
1 T cumin - ground
1 T oregano - dried
2 bay leaves
1 tsp cinnamon
1 T sugar
1C red wine - optional
5 chili piquins or 2 habeneros (both optional - super hot!!)
5 C pinto beans - cooked (pressure cooked, sidebar pg. 51)
2 tsp kosher salt
3 tsp fresh cracked pepper
1 bunch cilantro (cleaned and chopped to add at the end)

Gluten Free Option:
Use a gluten free lager in place of stout. I like Green's®.
Don't use a pale ale, it will be too bitter.

Roasted Green Chiles -
I like to stockpile roasted green chilies from our Aspen Saturday Farmers Market or any local farmers market that roasts on site. I let them sit in their bags in the refrigerator overnight, then seed and peel skin off under cold running water. Always wear latex free rubber gloves! You will regret not using them!!! Freeze until needed.

Separately cook meat. When almost done cooking add the stout or GF lager and reduce until most of the liquid is evaporated.

Place olive oil, onions, celery, carrots and yellow peppers into a 3 gallon stock pot, sauté 8 minutes. Add cooked meat and the rest of the ingredients, except cilantro. I usually add more chili powder and salt, to taste. Bring to a low rolling boil and cook for 30 minutes. Stir occasionally to keep the bottom of the pot from burning.

Remove from heat and add cilantro.

Optional - Serve with sides of sour cream, grated cheddar cheese and chopped green onions.

Green Chili & Pork Tenderloin Soup GF & DF
With Roasted Green Chiles

Serves 12

3 T olive oil
2 pork tenderloins - organic, ¾" dice
1 large or 2 medium onions - medium dice
5 cloves garlic - minced
3 red potatoes - small dice
1 (28 oz can) tomatillos - pulse in food processor
4 cups roasted green chiles (sidebar pg. 50 - small diced, seeded and skinned or 2 (28 oz) can Hatch® diced green chiles
2 cups pinto beans - cooked (side bar)
2 tsp ground cumin
1 T dried oregano or 3 T fresh - finely chopped
10 C chicken stock
1 bunch cilantro - coarsely chopped
2 bunches green onions - ⅛" thin round slices
S & P

In a separate pan sauté pork - sear in olive oil until browned and cooked. Set aside.

Place olive oil and onions into a 2 gallon stock pot, sauté 8 minutes. Add garlic, sauté one more minute. Add potatoes, tomatillos, green chiles, pinto beans, cumin, oregano, cooked pork and chicken stock. Bring to simmer to cook potatoes.

At the end of cooking, finish the soup by adding the green onions and cilantro. Add S & P to taste.

Vegan Option:
Use a no-chicken base. Omit the pork. Add 1 more potato and 1C more pinto beans.

Pressure Cook Pinto Beans -
Sort and rinse beans, making sure to pick out loose stones or dirt. Cover beans with at least 3" of water. Bring pressure cooker to noise for 25 minutes. Take off heat and let the pressure cooker release pressure on it's own. When the pressure valve button goes down, you can safely open your pressure cooker. I find that pressure cooking beans takes the gas out. I tend to make more than I will need, the extra will store well in the freezer.

"**Noise**" is the term for the noise the pressure cooker makes when pressure has built up and is cooking and releasing excess steam.

Chicken & Red Chili Posole
With Avocado and Baked Tortilla Strips

GF & DF

Serves 12

6 T olive oil
1 large onion- medium dice
3 cloves garlic - fine mince
8 C chicken stock
¼ C red chili sauce (pg 84) or 2 chipotle peppers canned in adobo sauce - fine dice
4 to 5 chicken breasts
2 C hominy - I use the 28 oz can
1 zucchini - cut into quarters length wise and ½ inch dice
1 bunch of kale - stemmed and thin slice
1 (28 oz) can diced tomatoes
2 T lime juice
1 bunch cilantro - loose chop
2 limes - cut into wedges, for garnish
2 avocados - sliced, for garnish
baked corn tortilla strips - for garnish

Sauté chicken breast in 3 T olive oil on medium heat, cover with lid while cooking. Flip and brown on other side. Depending on size of breast, it could take up to 8 minutes per side. When done thinly slice on the diagonal. Set aside.

Place remaining 3 T olive oil and onions into a 2 gallon stock pot, sauté 8 minutes. Add garlic, chicken stock, red chili sauce, sliced chicken breasts, hominy, zucchini, kale, diced tomatoes and lime juice. Simmer until heated through and zucchini is cooked, about 10-15 minutes.

Top with sliced avocados, cilantro and baked tortilla strips (below).

Baked Tortilla Strips
1 pkg of corn tortillas
¼ C olive oil
S & P

Heat oven to 350°. Slice corn tortillas into ¼" strips and coat with olive oil, using a pastry brush. Add salt and pepper, to taste. Place on a parchment lined sheet pan and bake until crispy, about 10-15 minutes.

Cindy's Homemade Chicken Stock
With Chicken Dumpling Soup

I usually stockpile leftover chicken bones from dinner, along with some of the juices or sauce. I keep adding them to a Ziploc® bag in the freezer until I need them for stock. These add more flavor to your basic stock. Be aware, homemade stocks become gelatinous in the refrigerator. The consistency will thin with re-heat.

Homemade Chicken Stock - *Serves 12* ❄ GF & DF
2 whole chickens cut into quarters along with extra
    bones from freezer
The cut off ends and leafy parts of celery from below recipe
The cut off ends and peels of carrots from below recipe
1 onion - cut in half plus ends and skin from below recipe
The stems of the parsley from below recipe
1 T black peppercorns
3 bay leaves

In a 5 gallon stock pot cover above ingredients with water. Bring to a boil, then reduce to low rolling boil. Cook about 2 hours. Take the chicken out and let cool down. Remove meat and shred with your fingers. Set aside. Put bones back into the stock and continue cooking, reducing stock 3 more hours. Strain the stock and set aside. Save extra bits of good chicken and discard all remaining solids. Add the shredded chicken to stock.

Chicken Dumpling Soup - *Serves 12*
3 T olive oil
10 carrots - peeled, thinly sliced on the rounds
1 bunch celery - small dice
1 large onion - small diced
1 T fresh sage - fine chop
1 T fresh thyme - fine chop
1 T fresh oregano - fine chop
16 C Homemade Chicken Stock with meat, from above recipe
¼ C Italian parsley - coarsely chopped
1 bunch green onions - thinly sliced on the diagonal
S & P
Dumplings - see sidebar (Omit for GF & DF)

Place olive oil, carrots, celery and onions into a 2 or 3 gallon stock pot, sauté 8 minutes. Add sage, thyme, oregano and Homemade Chicken Stock with meat (add extra store bought chicken stock if you don't have enough). Cook on a low rolling boil for 30-40 minutes. Add parsley and green onions and cook 5 minutes longer. Add S & P to taste.

Cook Dumplings separately and add to finished chicken soup. Serve.

Gluten Free/Dairy Free Option:
In place of Dumplings: Use 2 medium red potatoes - small dice. Cook with the rest of the veggies. Or 1½ C cooked wild rice and ½ C cooked jasmine rice, add at the end of soup.

Dumplings - (this is NOT GF or DF)
1 C milk - scald. Add 3 T flour, 3 T sugar, ½ tsp salt, 1 egg. Mix until thick, you may need an additional ½ C flour to get the right consistency. Drop by spoonfuls into boiling chicken stock, cover and reduce to simmer with lid on for 20 minutes. Add to chicken soup and serve immediately.

Collections from an Aspen Chef ~ Cindy Rogers

Di Baby's Vegan Chili
With Roasted Green Chiles, Beans and Quinoa

❄ GF, DF & VG

This is my version of my friend Di Baby's yummy vegan chili, she uses more yellow and red peppers than I do. If you like peppers, by all means add more. Always check labels, some tempeh burgers contain wheat grain.

Serves 12

2 to 3 T olive oil
1 large onion - medium dice
½ bunch celery - medium dice
6 carrots - diced
1 yellow pepper - medium dice
2 cloves garlic - minced
1 GF tempeh burger - diced in ¼" cubes (slice off edges if they are discolored)
3 C pinto beans - cooked (pressure cooked, sidebar pg. 51)
½ C quinoa - uncooked
8 C veggie stock
1 C green chiles - roasted and diced (farmers market, or canned Hatch® green chiles)
2 (28 oz) cans diced tomatoes
1 T oregano
2 tsp cumin
¼ tsp cayenne
S & P

Place olive oil, onions, celery and carrots into a 2 gallon stock pot, sauté 8 minutes. Add garlic and yellow pepper and sauté 1 minute more. Add stock, cooked pinto beans, diced tempeh burgers, quinoa and spices. Cook on low until quinoa is cooked, about ½ hour. Di Baby cooks her quinoa ahead of time and adds the amount she wants to her soup. Either way is good.

Can be served with corn tortilla chips.

Filé Gumbo
With Andouille Sausage, Chicken & Shrimp

❄ GF & DF

Serves 12

3 to 4 T olive oil
2 onions - medium dice
8 stalks celery - medium dice
2 green bell peppers diced or 1 (28 oz) can roasted green chiles
1 T Tabasco®
5 cloves garlic - minced
2 (28 oz) cans tomato sauce
2 (28 oz) cans diced tomatoes
8 C chicken stock
8 chicken thighs, boneless and skinless - large chop
2 lbs andouille sausage or chorizo sausage
1 lb medium shrimp - peeled and deveined

Seasoning Mix:
3 T filé gumbo
1 tsp kosher salt or more to taste
1 tsp white pepper
1 tsp black pepper
1 tsp oregano
1 tsp thyme
1 tsp cayenne
1 ½ tsp paprika

> **Filé powder -**
> Filé powder is a spicy herb made from the dried and ground leaves of the Sassafras tree. It's made from grinding sassafras leaves and stems into a powder. Filé is used as a thickening agent for gumbo and other Creole dishes, adding a distinctive earthy flavor.

Prepare seasoning mix. Set aside. Sauté the onions, celery and peppers in olive oil over medium heat. (If using green chiles, add with tomatoes and chicken stock.) Stir in seasoning mix, Tabasco®, and garlic. Cook 4-5 minutes, stirring constantly with a flat wooden spatula to make the roux. To make sure it doesn't burn, use your flat spatula to scrape the bottom of the pan. Stir in tomato sauce, diced tomatoes and chicken stock. Add chicken thighs and cook 45 minutes to one hour on medium low. Slice andouille sausage on the diagonal and brown in a separate pan on both sides, add to the gumbo. If using chorizo, crumble and sauté until cooked thoroughly, add to the gumbo. This soup can be prepared up to 2 days ahead or frozen at this stage.

Add shrimp before serving and cook 5 minutes, until done. Serve Filé Gumbo over rice.

Rice
2 C water
1 C Jasmine Rice

Your choice of rice. I would use jasmine with a ratio of 2 parts water to 1 part rice. Bring to a boil, add rice and stir. Cover and simmer for 20 minutes. Fluff with a fork and serve.

Caramelized Onion Soup
With Gruyere Crostini

Serves 12

4 T butter
6 yellow onions - cut into ¼" half circles
1 T sugar
2 T flour
½ C dry sherry
8 C beef stock
2 T fresh thyme
¼ tsp fresh cracked pepper

Melt butter in a large sauté pan, add onions, sugar, salt and pepper. Sauté on low heat, for about 1 hour until caramelized. Stir often. Onions will start to brown quickly towards the end, watch them closely so they don't burn. Toss flour on onions and stir to coat. Add sherry and 3 cups of beef stock, whisking constantly until incorporated. Transfer to a 2 gallon stock pot and add remaining beef stock, pepper, and thyme, Cook until flavors meld, about 15 minutes. Add salt to taste, sometimes the beef stock will be salty enough.

Crostini (glossary pg 182)
1 French baguette - sliced crosswise
8 oz Gruyere cheese - grated
2 T butter and 2 T olive oil - melted

Preheat oven to 350°. Parchment line a sheet pan and place sliced baguette pieces. Brush olive oil and butter mix on baguette pieces, toast until crisp - about 10 minutes.

To serve – Ladle soup into oven safe soup bowls. Top with 2 crostini, then sprinkle on Gruyere cheese and broil until cheese is melted and crispy. Check every 5 minutes to make sure they don't burn.

Dairy Free Option:
Use olive oil in place of butter and either use a vegan cheese or omit the cheese on the crostini. If you can tolerate goat cheese, use a hard goat gouda grated and melted on the crostini.

Gluten Free Option:
For the Crostini use a gluten free baguette. For the soup use 1 T arrowroot in place of flour. Don't add arrowroot to the onions. In stead add to ¼ C cold water. Mix with a fork and add with the stock to the soup.

Puréed Carrot Ginger Soup
With Candied Cashews

❄ **GF & DF**

Serves 12

2 T olive oil
1 onion - large dice
3 stalks of celery - small dice
10 carrots - peeled and chopped in a food processor
2 sweet potatoes - peeled and medium dice
2-3 T fresh ginger - finely grated
8 C chicken stock
1 C fresh orange juice
¼ tsp nutmeg - whole, finely grate
⅛ tsp white pepper
2 C coconut milk in the carton (pg. 10)
1 C candied cashews (for garnish - optional)
S & P

Place olive oil, onions, celery and carrots into a 2 gallon stock pot, sauté 8 minutes. Add sweet potato, ginger, chicken stock, orange juice, nutmeg, white pepper and cook for 40 minutes, until veggies are tender. Add coconut milk. Add S & P to taste.

Purée with soup-wand or blender (side bar).

This soup will separate, just give a stir and enjoy.

Candied Cashews
2 C unsalted cashews - whole (peanut oil free, check label)
4 C boiling water
⅔ C powdered sugar
1 tsp kosher salt
2 pinches cayenne
2 pinches chile powder

Drop nuts into boiling water and boil 30 seconds, drain. Toss nuts in powdered sugar, salt and spices. Bake at 350° on foil-lined sheet pan until golden brown, about 10-20 minutes. Keep checking the nuts so they don't burn.

Vegan Option:
Use a no-chicken base stock in place of chicken stock.

Soup Wand or Immersion Blender vs Blender -
Soup wand, aka immersion blender, is my tool of choice. I use it to blend soups right in the pot they were prepared in. If you use an upright blender, make sure the clear ingredient cup on the top of the lid is removed, leaving an open hole. Otherwise it will explode and make a huge mess. You can use a dish cloth to cover the hole to keep the spatter down.

Whole Nutmeg -
To finely grate whole nutmeg use a nutmeg grater. They are easy to find online. Freshly grated nutmeg goes a long way and is worth the effort.

Ribollita Soup
Thick Tuscan Soup

Traditionally this Tuscan soup has stale bread added at the end to thicken it. I like it without, it's thick enough with all of the veggies and you can eliminate the gluten.

❄ GF

Serves 12

1 lb Italian sausage (hot or sweet, your preference)
2 to 3 T olive oil
1 yellow onion - small dice
3 leeks - white and light green parts only - cleaned, ¼" thinly slice (see sidebar for cleaning)
6 stalks celery - small dice
4 carrots - peeled, small dice
½ head Savory or Napa cabbage - thinly slice
8 to10 small fingerling potatoes - scrubbed and ¼" slice
1 large sweet potato - peeled, small dice
3 cloves garlic - minced
2 T Italian parsley - coarsely chopped
1 T fresh marjoram or 3 tsp dried marjoram
1 (28 oz) can diced tomatoes
2 C cooked cannellini or navy beans
8 C chicken stock
2 zucchini - cut lengthwise into quarters, thinly slice ¼"
1 bunch Tuscan kale - remove rib, thinly slice
1 bunch Swiss chard - remove thick rib only, thinly slice
S & P
¼ C Parmesan cheese - finely grate, for garnish
¼ C basil - chiffonade, for garnish

Dairy Free Option: Omit the Parmesan cheese garnish.

Vegan Option: Omit Italian sausage and Parmesan cheese garnish. Use a vegetable Base or no-chicken base, in place of the chicken stock.

Cleaning Leeks - Cut off root end. Cut green off 1 to 2" above white. I usually have a 5" segment left. Cut the trimmed leek in half lengthwise and run under cold water until the dirt is removed. Check in between layers to see that all the dirt is gone.

Cook the Italian sausage in a sauté pan until done. Set aside.

Place olive oil, onions, leeks, celery and carrots into a 2 gallon stock pot, sauté 8 minutes. Add cabbage, potatoes, sweet potatoes, garlic, Italian parsley, marjoram, diced tomatoes, beans and chicken stock. At a low rolling boil, cook the soup until potatoes are fork tender, about 30-40 minutes. Add the cooked Italian sausage and zucchini, cook 5 minutes. Add the Swiss chard and kale and cook 5 minutes longer. Add S & P to taste.

Garnish with Parmesan cheese and basil.

Potato Leek Soup
With Coconut Milk

GF & DF

Serves 12

2 T olive oil
1 onion - medium dice
9 leeks - white and light green parts only - cleaned, ¼" thinly slice (see sidebar for cleaning leeks)
10 red potatoes - medium dice, skin on, scrubbed clean
10 C chicken stock
4 C coconut milk in the carton (pg. 10)
¼ C Italian parsley - coarsely chopped
S & P

Place olive oil, onions and leeks into a 2 gallon stock pot, sauté 5 minutes. Add chicken stock and potatoes. Cook at a low rolling boil until the potatoes fork tender, about 30-40 minutes. (Use a fork to insert into potato, if it falls apart, it's done.) Add coconut milk. Purée soup for 30 seconds, you want it to be chunky. Add the parsley.
Add S & P to taste.

Vegan Option: Use no-chicken base in place of chicken stock

Cleaning Leeks - Cut off root end. Cut green off 1 to 2" above white. I usually have a 5" segment left. Cut the trimmed leek in half lengthwise and run under cold water until the dirt is removed. Check in between layers to see that all the dirt is gone.

Soup Wand or Immersion Blender vs Blender - Soup wand, aka immersion blender, is my tool of choice. I use it to blend soups right in the pot they were prepared in. If you use an upright blender, make sure the clear ingredient cup on the top of the lid is removed, leaving an open hole. Otherwise it will explode and make a huge mess. You can use a dish cloth to cover the hole to keep the spatter down.

Vegan Lentil Soup
With Crushed Red Pepper

❄ GF, DF & VG

My sister-in-law Jonsie, used to make a delicious lentil soup. This is my version of her healthy soup.

Serves 12
2 T olive oil
1 medium onion - small dice
½ bunch celery - clean, small diced
3 carrots - sliced into thin rounds
2 medium red potatos or 1 sweet potato - medium dice
1 (28 oz) can diced tomatoes
2 C lentils
12 cups vegetable stock
1 T crushed red pepper
1 T chili powder
1 tsp ground cumin
S & P

Place olive oil, onions, celery and carrots into a 2 gallon stock pot, sauté 5 minutes. Add the rest of the ingredients, except the salt. (Use salt to finish the soup at the end of cooking. I find that most stocks have enough salt, you may not need to add any.)

Bring soup to a boil and reduce to a medium simmer for 2 to 3 hours. You may need to add water to the pot if the soup reduces too much.

French Sorrel Soup
With Potatoes and Leeks

❄ **GF & DF**

This is one of my favorite summer soups. My friend Sallyanne gave me a recipe out of her cooking files years ago, similar to this one. French sorrel is hard to find in the grocery store, so I grow it in my vegetable garden. It grows as a perennial and if you harvest it early enough, sometimes you can get a second cutting.

Serves 12

2 T olive oil
3 leeks - cleaned and sliced thin (sidebar pg. 59)
8 C chicken stock
4 medium red potatoes - diced, skin on
8 C French sorrel - firmly packed and stems removed
1 lemon - juiced
coconut milk in the carton, see pg. 10 - (optional)
S & P

Place olive oil and leeks into a 2 gallon stock pot, sauté 5 minutes. Add potatoes and chicken stock. Cook until potatoes are fork tender, about 30-40 minutes. Add French sorrel and cook another 5 minutes. Add S & P to taste.

Blend with a soup wand until puréed.

If you choose to use the coconut milk, add it now.

This soup is good served cold or hot. If it separates in the refrigerator, just give it a good stir and enjoy.

Vegan Option: Use a no-chicken base stock in place of chicken stock.

Soup Wand or Immersion Blender vs. Blender - Soup wand, aka immersion blender, is my tool of choice. I use it to blend soups right in the pot they were prepared in. If you use an upright blender, make sure the clear ingredient cup on the top of the lid is removed, leaving an open hole. Otherwise it will explode and make a huge mess. You can use a dish cloth to cover the hole to keep the spatter down.

Chunky Gazpacho
With Farm Fresh Tomatoes

GF, DF & VG

This is the version of Gazpacho I wrote after my former husband Toms' parents gave us a case of beautiful tomatoes from their garden. They were all ripening at the same time so i made this yummy cold soup with the delicious garden fresh tomatoes. I prefer my gazpacho chunky, but some like it puréed.

Serves 12

2 cucumbers
2 bunches green onion
8-10 medium tomatoes - small dice -(I like to mix the Early Girl tomatoes with some heirlooms from the farmers market, or use your favorites from your garden)
1 yellow pepper - small dice
1-2 cloves garlic - minced
1 tsp kosher salt
½ C sherry vinegar
½ tsp fresh cracked pepper
5 C V8® juice
8-10 drops Tabasco®
1 bunch Italian parsley - stemmed, loosely chopped
1 avocado and 2 limes - for garnish

Peel the cucumbers. Cut in half and use a spoon to scoop out seeds. Small dice and add to a large bowl. Clean the green onions under running water and cut the root ends off. Use the white of the onion, along with the good looking green parts (discard the rest) and thinly slice on the diagonal. Add to the bowl. Add the remaining ingredients and mix well. Let the flavors meld overnight or at least 6 hours. Garnish each bowl with 3 slices of avocado and a lime wedge. Serve.

Classic Split Pea Soup
With Leftover Ham

❄ GF & DF

This is a great soup to make with your leftover spiral cut ham from Thanksgiving or Christmas.

Serves 12

2 T olive oil
1 yellow onion - small dice
½ bunch celery - small dice
3 carrots - peeled, chop fine (I like to pulse in a food processor to a fine chop)
2 T fresh thyme
2 ham hocks or leftover picnic ham, or spiral cut ham with the bones
1 bag dried green split peas
S & P
10 C water (approximately)

Place olive oil, onions, celery, carrots and thyme into a 2 gallon stock pot, sauté 8 minutes. Add split peas and ham and cover with 3" of water. Bring to a boil. Turn heat to a simmer and cook until peas are soft (about 2 hours). Keep checking the water level and add more as needed. The cooking time depends on the freshness of the peas. When peas are soft, remove ham meat and bone from the soup. Discard bone, cartilage and fat. Cut up ham and return to the soup. Continue cooking until the soup is a thick consistancy, (about another half hour). Stiring frequently. Season with S & P to taste.

Collections from an Aspen Chef
Favorite recipes with options to accommodate your dietary preferences

GF = Gluten Free ~ DF = Dairy Free ~ VG = Vegan ~ ❄ = Freezes Well

Collections from an Aspen Chef
Favorite recipes with options to accommodate your dietary preferences

Sides:

Roasted Brussels Sprouts w/Lemon & Bacon	66
Southwestern Corn Bread	67
Corn Bread Stuffing w/Chorizo & Dried Fruit	68
Bourbon Baked Beans	69
Charra Beans, Texas Style Pintos	70
Farrotto, Spelt Risotto with Asparagus & Peas	71
Wild Rice & Wheat Berry Pilaf	72
Quinoa Melange in Carrot Juice	73
Creamy Polenta & Spicy Sprouted Beans	74
Roasted Fennel, Apples, Beets & Leeks	75
Baked Potato Fries & Mashers	76
Veggie Burgers w/Pinto Beans	77
Southwestern Corn Salad	78
Hot Yeast Rolls	79
Gluten Free Buttermilk Biscuits	80
Gluten Free Pizza Dough	81

Roasted Brussels Sprouts
With Lemon & Bacon

GF & DF

This dish has changed the minds of dubious Brussels sprouts eaters.

Serves 12
2 lbs Brussels sprouts
1 lb bacon - fried and crumbled
1 lemon - zest and juice
¼ C extra virgin olive oil
S & P

> **Vegan Option:** Omit the bacon, it's still delicious.

Preheat oven to 350°.
Use a single piece of heavy duty foil that is twice ths size of a sheet pan. Spread half of the foil over the sheet pan, the other half will overlap the Brussels sprouts to create a baking pouch on the sheet pan.

Cut off ends of Brussels sprouts and remove blemished outer layer. Then thinly slice, about ⅛".

Add sliced Brussels sprouts and lemon zest to foil lined sheet pan. Then add 2 T to ¼ C olive oil to thoroughly coat. Add S & P to taste. Hold edges of foil together and fold in to create a baking pouch.

Bake for 45 minutes to 1 hour. After 35 minutes check to see if Brussels sprouts are done. They should be soft with crunchy pieces around the edges.

When Brussels sprouts are done, place on a platter, add bacon and reserved lemon juice. Toss and serve.

Southwestern Cornbread
With Green Chile Peppers

Serves 10

1 C butter
¾ C sugar
4 eggs
1 C cornmeal - fine or medium
1 C flour
2 T baking powder
1 tsp kosher salt
½ C pepper jack cheese - grated
1½ C cream style corn
½ C roasted green chiles - diced

> **Guten Free Option:**
> Use 2 C cornmeal and omit the flour.

Preheat oven to 350°.

In a mixer, cream butter and sugar. Add eggs one at a time. Add cornmeal, flour, baking powder, and salt. Stir until combined. Add cheese, cream style corn and green chiles.

Bake in a greased and floured 13 x 9 pan for 45 minutes to 1 hour.

Holiday Cornbread Stuffing
With Chorizo & Dried Fruit

GF

Mrs. B's Skillet Cornbread - *Serves 12*
3 T olive oil
1 lg egg
2 C cornmeal
2 C buttermilk
4 T sugar
½ tsp kosher salt
4 tsp baking powder

Dairy Free Option: For the cornbread use coconut milk in the carton, in place of the buttermilk.

Preheat oven to 350°. Heat 3 T olive oil in a 10" cast iron skillet in the oven, for 5 minutes. Mix the rest of the ingredients in a bowl and pour into the preheated skillet. Bake for 20 minutes or until golden brown on top. Take out and flip out of skillet onto sheet pan.

Holiday Cornbread Stuffing − *serves 12*
Mrs. B's cornbread (above recipe)
½ C dried cherries
½ C dried apricots - medium dice
½ C slivered almonds
2 T olive oil
4 celery stalks - medium dice
3 carrots - medium dice
1 onion - medium dice
1 lb chorizo sausage
2 eggs - optional
1 tsp cumin
2 tsp oregano
½ C chicken stock to soften cornbread
S & P

Dairy Free Option: For the chorizo, make sure there is no dairy, including casien. There are brands of sausages and chroizo that contain casien and sometimes milk. Always check labels.

Cube Mrs. B's cornbread into 1" pieces - dry in a 350° oven on a sheetpan for 10 - 20 minutes, turning often. When cooled put into a large bowl and add cherries, apricots and slivered almonds. Set aside.
Sauté the celery, carrots and onions in olive oil, until onions are translucent, Add to the cornbread mixture.
Sauté chorizo in a skillet until it's cooked and browned. Add to the cornbread mix.
Add eggs and seasoning to the cornbread mixture and stir thoroughly. Add chicken stock to moisten the stuffing, about ¼ C at a time. You will probably only need ½ C or less. You want your stuffing moist.

Add stuffing to turkey, pg 104. Follow baking instructions.

Bourbon Baked Beans
With Bacon

GF & DF

This is a great dish to serve with Baby back ribs with hoison glaze pg. 120 and southwestern corn salad pg. 78.

Serves 12

2 lbs bacon
2 yellow onions - diced
8 cloves garlic - minced
2 C ketchup
1 C molasses
1 C Dijon mustard
1 C bourbon or whiskey (I use Jack Daniels®)
8 T brown sugar
8 T Worcestershire® sauce
12 dashes Tabasco®
6 (28 oz) cans Bush's® baked beans
S & P

Preheat oven to 350°.
Cook bacon. Crumble and set aside. Reserve ⅓ C bacon for garnish and 3 T bacon grease for sauté. In a Dutch oven (or an oven safe pot), sauté onions in 3 T of bacon grease until translucent. Add garlic and cook 1 minute. Then add ketchup, molasses, Dijon mustard, bourbon, brown sugar, Worcestershire® sauce and Tabasco® - simmer 5 minutes. Open cans of Bush's® beans and rinse beans under cold water. Remove pork fat chunks. Add beans to the rest of the ingredients and bake for 1½ hours, covered.

Gluten Free WARNING: Some experts say that the distillation process removes harmful gluten proteins from alcohol. Some experts advise using only alcohol made from non-gluten grain sources. Use your own judgement if you are allergic to gluten. Some alcohol distilleries might add caramel color which can contain gluten.

Fish Allergies - Worcestershire® sauce has anchovies. Check label for GF, Lee & Perrins® is GF. Omit and replace with tamari if you need to.

Charra Beans, Texas Style Pintos
With Bacon & Zing

GF & DF

I had some clients from Texas who inspired me to come up with my rendition of Charra or drunken beans.

Serves 8 - 10

1 lb bacon – diced
1 yellow onion – diced
4 C pinto beans - cooked (pressure cooked, sidebar)
⅓ C sliced pickled jalapeno peppers – diced
2 lg tomatoes - diced
¼ C tequila
2 tsp cumin
1 tsp kosher salt
2 tsp chili powder
1 bunch of cilantro - chopped
1 bunch of green onions - chopped

Sauté bacon. Crumble and set aside. Reserve 3 T bacon grease. Sauté onion in bacon grease until translucent. Add pinto beans, pickled jalapenos, tomatoes, tequila, cumin and chili powder. Simmer about 10 minutes or until the tequila is reduced. Remove from heat, stir in bacon, cilantro and green onions. Serve.

If you want a cheater recipe (quicker prep)

4 C pinto beans - canned or pressure cooked (sidebar)
1 lb bacon - cooked and crumbled
⅓ C pickled jalapenos - diced
1 (7 oz) can Herdez Salsa Casera®
1 (7 oz) can Herdez Salsa Verde®
1 bunch green onions - washed and chopped
1 bunch cilantro - washed and chopped

Combine cooked pinto beans, cooked bacon (no grease), jalapenos and salsas. Cook for 15 minutes. Add green onions and cilantro at the end. If using cheese, add now. Serve.

Vegan Option:
Omit bacon.

Cheesy Option:
You can add grated pepper jack cheese on top of the charra beans in the serving bowl and melt to make a great cheesy bean dip.

Pressure Cook Pinto Beans -
Sort and rinse beans, making sure to pick out loose stones or dirt. Cover beans with at least 3" of water. Bring pressure cooker to noise for 25 minutes. Take off heat and let the pressure cooker release pressure on it's own. When the pressure valve button goes down, you can safely open your pressure cooker. I find that pressure cooking beans takes the gas out. I tend to make more than I will need, the extra will store well in the freezer.

Farrotto - a.k.a. Spelt Risotto
With Asparagus, Mushrooms & Peas

Farro is sometimes refered to as Spelt. It's a wheat grain and does contain gluten. Farrotto is cooked like rissotto only made with the farro grain instead of Arborio rice.

Serves 8 - 10

4 T olive oil
2 C farro - soaked in water for at least 4 hours
¼ C white wine
10 crimini mushrooms - washed, thinly sliced
4 cloves garlic - minced
2 bunches green onions - finely chopped
6 C chicken stock
2 bunchs asparagus - blanched (tips and 1" of stem)
1 C frozen peas
1 C grated Parmesan cheese - finely grated
½ C Italian parsley - coarsely chopped

Dairy Free Option: Omit the Parmesan cheese, it's still delicious.

Saute mushrooms in 2 T olive oil. Add garlic and green onions, mix well and sauté one minute, set aside.

Drain farro and sauté in 2 T olive oil for 3 minutes, stir to coat. Deglaze skillet with ¼ C of white wine. Stir until absorbed. Add 2 C chicken stock, sautéed mushrooms, garlic and green onions; reduce until the farro has absorbed the liquid. Continue adding ½ C at a time until absorbed, stirring frequently. When you see the bottom of the pan add ½ C more stock. When the farro becomes soft and chewy, finish with ¼ C more stock, blanched asparagus, peas. When liquid is absorbed, add Parmesan cheese and parsley (save ¼ C of each parsley and Parmesan cheese to add to the top as garnish). Serve.

Wild Rice Pilaf
With Wheat Berries, Jasmine Rice & Almonds

DF

Serves 8 - 10

½ C wild rice
½ C wheat berries
4 C chicken stock
¼ C jasmine rice
¼ C tamari almonds - chopped
¼ C parsley - chopped
3 T olive oil or coconut oil
S & P

Soak the wild rice and wheat berries in water for 2 hours. Drain. Bring 4 C chicken stock with wild rice/wheat berry mix to boil. Reduce to a simmer for 30 minutes - uncovered.

Add ¼ C Jasmine rice, cover and simmer for 20 minutes.
(if there is still some liquid after this, boil until it's reduced down, or drain if there is a lot of liquid.)

Add olive oil or coconut oil, chopped tamari almonds and parsley.

Vegan Option: In place of chicken stock, use a vegetable base or no-chicken base.

Guten Free Option: Omit the wheat berries and use 1 C wild rice.

Quinoa Melange in Carrot Juice
With Stir Fry Zucchini & Caramelized Onions

GF, DF & VG

A client of mine gave me the idea of cooking quinoa in carrot juice, she used a mix of carrot juice and stock. I use only carrot juice to make the quinoa richer.

Serves 8 - 10
4 C carrot juice
2 C quinoa
2 carrots - peel and thinly slice into rounds

Bring carrot juice to boil. Add quinoa and carrots. Simmer uncovered for 25 minutes. Set aside at room temperature.

Caramelized Onions
3 onions - thinly sliced
2 T olive oil
2 T sugar
1 tsp kosher salt

Sauté onions in olive oil, sugar and salt. Cook on low for half an hour to one hour or until the onions turn golden brown and are caramelized. Set aside.

Toasted Pine Nuts
¼ C pine nuts

Add nuts to dry sauté pan on medium heat. Stir until the nuts start to brown. Keep an eye on them - they can burn very quickly. Remove from heat. Place into a bowl and set aside.

Sautéd Zucchini
1 T olive oil
2 zucchini - small dice
1 tsp dried marjoram or 1 T fresh - finely chopped
1 bunch green onions - thinly slice on the diagonal

Cut zucchini lengthwise into quarters, then slice along the round to get pie-shaped pieces. Sauté in olive oil with marjoram until brown. Add green onions. Combine cooked quinoa, sautéd zucchini and caramelized onions. Sprinkle with toasted pine nuts. Serve.

Collections from an Aspen Chef ~ Cindy Rogers

Creamy Polenta & Spicy Sprouted Beans
With or without Cheese

Serves 8   **GF**

1 C polenta - coarse or medium grit
4 C water
½ C grated Parmesan cheese or Manchego cheese
2 T coconut oil (pg. 10) or olive oil
S & P

Bring 4 cups of water to boil. Add 1 cup of polenta. Stir and continue cooking on medium low heat, until polenta thickens, about 10 minutes. Take off heat and add coconut oil or olive oil, and cheese.
S & P to taste.

Spicy Sprouted Beans   GF, DF & VG

2 C dried beans- (a mix of mung beans, black eyed peas, garbonzo beans, and adzuki beans)
water
2 tsp chili powder
1 tsp cumin
½ tsp black pepper
1 tsp kosher salt
1 T coconut oil, pg 10

Cover and soak beans in cold water overnight. Strain and rinse. Drain beans through a piece of cheesecloth set in a strainer. Leave cheesecloth, beans and strainer on top of a bowl to catch the extra water. Rinse twice a day, the beans should start to sprout on the second or third day. You can eat them raw at this stage.

Or...
Rinse beans and place in a pan. Cover with about 2" water. Add all the spices except the salt. Bring to a low boil and cook for 40 minutes. Check the water level. You want about a ½ inch of cooking liquid remaining with the beans after they are cooked. You can add water to the beans while they are cooking if needed. When done, add salt and coconut oil.

These two dishes are great together as side dishes or with grilled veggies or a salad as a main course.

Dairy Free & Vegan Option:
Omit Parmesan cheese.

Note on Polenta -
Basically polenta is a type of ground corn meal. Fine or medium grit is usually used for polenta. There is a coarse ground also. (Grits are made from ground white corn or ground hominy.)

Note on Bean Mix -
I like to keep a big jar of mixed beans in my cupboard. I buy small bags of mung beans, black-eyed peas, garbanzos beans and adzuki. Mix them all together so they are ready when you need them.

Roasted Fennel, Apples & More
With Roasted Cauliflower and Asparagus as Sides

GF, DF & VG

Serves 8
3 T olive oil
3 fennel bulbs - large julienne
2 red onions - large julienne
3 Fuji apples - large julienne
3 beets - peeled small wedges
2 lg sweet potatoes or yams - peeled and 1" cube

Preheat oven to 425°.
Toss all of the above ingredients in olive oil, S & P to taste.
Roast for 35 to 45 minutes until done, flipping once or twice to keep from burning.

Roasted Cauliflower
1 head of cauliflower
2 T olive oil
S & P

Preheat oven to 425°.
Foil line a sheet pan. Cut cauliflower into little florets, add to sheet pan and toss with olive oil, S & P to taste. Roast in a 425° oven until golden brown - about 35 minutes. Flip once or twice to prevent burning.

Roasted Asparagus
2 bunches asparagus - cut woody ends off
2 T olive oil
S & P

Preheat oven to broil.
Place asparagus on a sheet pan, coat with olive oil, S & P to taste.

Broil for 5 minutes, check the oven to make sure they don't burn. When they are browned, take out of the oven, platter and serve.

Baked Fries & Mashed Potatoes

With Sweet potatoes and Red potatoes

GF, DF & VG

Potato Fries - *Serves 8 - 10*
5 medium red potatoes
2 to 3 T olive oil
Cajun Seasoning pg. 93

Preheat oven to 350°. Scrub potatoes and slice into french fries. Add to sheet pan and toss in olive oil to lightly coat. Add a sprinkling of Cajun Seasoning. Toss by hand. Bake for 20 minutes, flip and bake another 20 minutes until golden brown.

Sweet Potato Fries - *Serves 8 - 10*
3 medium sweet potatoes or yams - peeled
1 to 2 T olive oil
Cajun Seasoning pg. 93

Preheat oven to 425°. Peel sweet potatoes. Slice into large french fries. Add to foil lined sheet pan and toss in olive oil to lightly coat. Add a sprinkling of Cajun Seasoning. Toss by hand.

Bake for 20 minutes, flip and bake another 20 minutes or until they start to brown.

Vegan Mashed Potatoes - *Serves 8 - 10*
8 red potatoes or yukon golds - peels on
¼ C coconut oil - pg 10
½ -1 C coconut milk - in the carton, pg 10
S & P

Scrub potatoes under running water to clean. Cut into quarters. Boil until fork tender and drain. Add coconut oil and mash down with a potato masher. Add coconut milk in small increments to get the right consistency.

Veggie Burgers with Pinto Beans ❄ GF, DF & VG
With Southwestern Flair

Serves 6
½ yellow onion - small dice
1 clove garlic - minced
2 C cooked pinto beans - (pressure cooked, sidebar pg. 51)
¼ C parsley - finely chopped
3 green onions - finely chopped
¼ C cilantro - finely chopped
½ C Olathe® corn kernels - blanched (or organic frozen kernels - thawed)
1 jalapeno pepper - minced
3 green onions - minced
¼ C jasmine rice - cooked
1 tsp ground cumin
S & P

Filler-
¼ - ½ C crumbled rice crackers or vegan mashed potatoes, (pg. 76), depending on how moist the mix is.

Sauté yellow onion in olive oil until translucent. Add garlic and turn off heat. Add the rest of the ingredients, except the filler, and mix well. Add filler to bind the mix, starting with ¼ C. The mixture should hold together and not be too dry or too wet. Form into burger patties.

Sauté patties in olive oil, to brown on each side and warm the insides. You can hold these in a 225° oven to keep warm.

Raw patties freeze well. Put raw patties on wax paper-lined sheet pan, then into the freezer. After they are frozen you can stack them inside a Ziploc® bag.

Southwestern Corn Salad
With Colorado Sweet Olathe® Corn

GF, DF & VG

This makes a great side dish for summer barbecues when fresh corn is a sweet and wonderful treat. You can use your local fresh corn, if Olathe® isn't available.

Serves 6

12 ears Olathe® sweet corn, or 6 C organic frozen corn kernels - thawed
3 jalapenos - fine dice
1 red pepper - fine dice
6 green onions - thinly sliced on the diagonal
½ bunch cilantro - stemmed, coarsely chopped

Clean and boil the ears of corn for 2 to 3 minutes - don't over boil or they will get mushy. Cool. Hold corn cob upright with one end on a cutting board. Try to remove all the corn silk. With a sharp knife cut the kernels off and put into a bowl. Add the rest of the ingredients, then add the vinaigrette to taste.

Cilantro Vinaigrette
½ bunch cilantro - stemmed
1 clove garlic
2 tsp honey
3 tsp Dijon mustard
⅓ C rice wine vinegar
½ C olive oil
⅛ tsp fresh cracked pepper
½ tsp kosher salt

Pulse in a food processor until chopped and emulsified.

Hot Yeast Rolls
Holiday Yummy Pull-apart Rolls

DF

Makes 3½ dozen small rolls
1 T dry yeast
1 C warm water
1½ C coconut milk, pg 10 - lukewarm
½ C olive oil
½ C + 1 T sugar
2 eggs
1 tsp kosher salt
6½ C flour

> **Dairy Option:** Can use milk in place of coconut milk.

In a stand mixer using the paddle attachment, combine warm water, yeast and 1T sugar. Mix for 30 seconds. When yeast starts to bubble add the lukewarm coconut milk, olive oil, ½ C sugar, salt and eggs. Mix for 1 minute. Then, using the bread hook attachment, add flour and mix for 3 minutes. Grease a large bowl and add the dough. Cover with plastic and let rise. Punch the dough down. Place onto a floured cutting board and cut into small balls, about 3½ dozen. Place about ½" apart on a greased sheet pan with a lip. Let rolls rise until they double in size (about half an hour to an hour, depending on how warm your kitchen is). Bake at 375° for 20 minutes.

You can prep this 4-5 hours ahead of time. Keep the dough in the refrigerator while it rises, (in the bowl and on the sheet pan). Pull rolls out of the refrigerator one hour before baking.

Gluten Free Buttermilk Biscuits
With Dairy Free Option

 GF

Makes 15 biscuits

1 C potato starch
1 C rice flour
½ C cornstarch (check label for GF)
3½ tsp xanthan gum
2 T baking powder
½ tsp baking soda
1 tsp kosher salt
2 T sugar
10 T butter - softened
1½ C buttermilk

Dairy Free Option: Use coconut milk in the carton (pg.10) in place of buttermilk and Earth Balance® in place of butter.

Corn Free Option: Use tapioca flour in place of corn starch.

Preheat oven to 375°.
Mix all of the ingredients in a mixing bowl using a stand mixer. Form into 1½" to 2" balls. Bake on a parchment-lined sheet pan for 15-20 minutes, or until golden brown. These are great right out of the oven, but will hold for a few hours. Re-heat right before serving. Baked biscuits also freeze well.

Gluten Free Pizza Dough
Prep Ahead Dough

❄ GF, DF & VG

Makes 3 pizza doughs
1 T yeast
1¼ C warm water
3 C GF flour mix (1C brown rice flour, 1C white rice flour, 1 C tapioca flour)
½ tsp xanthan gum
1 tsp kosher salt
½ tsp baking powder
3 T sugar
1 T olive oil

Preheat oven to 350°.
In a stand mixer using the paddle attachment, mix yeast and water for 10 seconds. After it bubbles, add flour mix, xanthan gum, salt, baking powder, sugar, then olive oil. Mix for 1 minute.

The dough will be sticky. Form into 3 balls and flatten out on parchment paper, dusted with rice flour. Coat your hands with rice flour and push the dough out with your fingers to the size and thickness you want. You can bake on a pizza stone or parchment paper on a sheet pan.

Pre-bake for 25 to 30 minutes, until crust is set and lightly brown. Take out of oven and add sauces, cheese and toppings. Finish baking until the toppings are hot and the cheese is melted.

You can also bake the pizza dough ahead of time. If you are using them the same day, leave them on the counter covered in plastic after they cool. If not, freeze them in a Ziploc® bag for up to a month and bring out when you need them.

Collections from an Aspen Chef
Favorite recipes with options to accommodate your dietary preferences

Collections from an Aspen Chef
Favorite recipes with options to accommodate your dietary preferences

Mexican and Italian:

Cindy's Tamales	84
Janette's Green Chili Sauce	85
Laura's Red Chili Sauce	86
Guacamole	87
Enchiladas Sauce & Vegetarian Enchiladas	88
Mac N' Cheese	89
Penne à la Vodka	90
Tofu Stuffed Pasta Shells	91
Spaghetti Carbonara	92
Cajun Blackening Seasoning Mix	93

GF = Gluten Free ～ DF = Dairy Free ～ VG = Vegan ～ ❄ = Freezes Well

Cindy's Tamales
With Sauces to Follow

❄ GF

My Aunt Lydia, taught me how to make tamales as a teenager. They are a lot of work, but worth the effort! This is my rendition of her tamales. Lydia taught me a lot about cooking when I was a teenager, I loved helping her out in the kitchen.

Masa - *Approximately 50-60 tamales*
8 C masa harina (buy fresh, it tends to go rancid)
8 C Olathe® corn kernels or frozen organic corn kernels
3 to 4 C milk, or coconut milk in the carton (pg. 10)
8 tsp baking powder
1 T kosher salt
3 C grated cheese (I like 2 C goat feta and 1 C Manchego or 2 C pepper jack and 1 C Monterey jack; you can use whatever cheeses you like)
4 C diced roasted green chiles
1 lb butter or 1 C Earth Balance®
1 C lard

With pastry cutter or fork, cream the butter and lard. Add masa harina, baking powder and salt. Mix. Add 4 C corn to 2 C milk and puree in a food processor. Add to the masa. Add 4 C whole corn kernels, green chiles and cheese. Add milk to moisten (you might not need all of the milk). You want your masa to hold together - not crumble or be too soupy.

Slow Cooked Pork
❄ GF & DF

1 pork shoulder or pork butt, bone-in
chicken stock to cover pork in slow cooker
2 tsp crushed red pepper

Put pork shoulder, chicken stock and red pepper flakes in a slow cooker. Cook for at least 6 hours. Shred pork with a fork, place in a container with some of the liquid. Make a day ahead.

Assemble -
2 packages corn husks
1 lb feta or 1 pkg cotija cheese - crumbled
Laura's Red Chili Sauce (pg 86, use GF option if needed)
Masa and Slow Cooked Pork recipes (above)

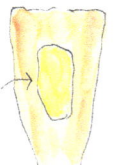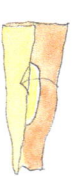

Soak larger corn husks in water to soften (tear off ¼" strips of smaller husks to tie off tamales). Lay 5 softened husks on a flat surface. Take ⅓ C of masa and place in the center of each corn husk. Add about 2 T cooked shredded pork. Top with 1 to 2 T Laura's Red Chili Sauce, and a little feta cheese or cotija crumbled on top. Fold in both sides, then tie off ends with thinly torn strips of corn husks. Continue with the remaining husks, and repeat until done.

Wrapped tamales can be either cooked or stored in the freezer.

Cook - Steam for 25 to 30 minutes, let rest for 10 minutes to firm up. Enjoy with Janette's Green Chili Sauce pg. 85 and Laura's Red Chili Sauce pg. 86. (Use GF option if needed)

Janette's Green Chili Sauce
With Farmers Market Roasted Green Chiles

 DF

This recipe is gladly shared by my friend Janette. She uses this sauce for amazing pork and green chili burritos. You can make a burrito by using her green chili sauce, slow cooked pork or shredded chicken, cheese, rice and pinto beans - wrap everything up in your favorite flour tortilla.

Makes about 8 C
3 T olive oil
4 to 6 cloves garlic - minced
8 C roasted green chiles or 5 quart-size bags from the farmers market
¼ C flour
3 - 4 C chicken stock
1 lemon - juiced
S & P

Gluten Free Option:
Use 1 T arrowroot mixed with 4 T chicken stock in place of flour. Add this with the chicken stock, and more if needed.

Vegan Option:
use vegetable stock in place of chicken stock.

Green Chili Prep
On Saturdays we have a wonderful farmers market in the Summer months in downtown Aspen. This is where I like to buy fresh roasted Anaheim or Big Jim green chiles; they are a medium heat. You can use any fresh roasted chiles. Let them sit in the plastic bags they come in for a few hours to sweat and release the skin. (I sometimes will leave them in the refrigerator overnight and clean them in the morning). Make sure you have latex-free gloves for this next part! Under cold running water (a slow stream) peel off the skins and remove stems and seeds from the chiles. You will regret not wearing gloves, especially if you touch your eyes! I've found that cleaning the chiles with water does not affect the heat of the chiles.

Green Chili Sauce
Chop green chiles and sauté in olive oil with garlic for about 5 minutes. Sprinkle flour on top of chiles, and stir with a flat wooden spatula. Whisk in 2 C chicken stock to incorporate the flour. Add garlic and the remaining 2 C chicken stock and cook until sauce thickens. If it's too thick add more stock. Finish the sauce with lemon juice.

I like to freeze this sauce in 1 to 2 C portions and thaw out when I need it. It's worth making a big batch and freezing.

Great over tamales, slow cooked pork or shredded chicken.

Shredded Chicken - Pressure Cooked
Take two to four chicken breasts and cover with 2 inches of chicken stock in a pressure cooker. Bring to noise for 15 minutes. Remove from heat and let cool down. When safe to open pressure cooker, drain the chicken stock and shred chicken with a fork. Add 1 C of Green chili sauce to shredded chicken and enjoy.

Laura's Red Chili Sauce
With New Mexican Red Chiles

❄ DF

This Recipe is shared by my friend, Laura. She introduced me to wonderful sauces combining flavors from New Mexico and India. This is a great sauce for meats & Mexican dishes.

Makes about 8 to 10 C
2 (8 oz) bags ancho chiles
2 (8 oz) bags guajilo chiles
2 (8 oz) bags New Mexico chiles
6 to 8 chipotle peppers
chicken stock to cover peppers

De-seed and remove stems from chiles. Put in a 2 gallon stock pot and cover with chicken stock. Boil on medium heat for half hour. Let cool. Add to a blender or food processor and puree. Then put through a strainer or chinois (a conical sieve with very fine mesh) to remove excess seeds and skin. I add some of the cooking liquid to the blender and to the strainer to help push pulp through. Don't throw the liquid away, use it as you blend and strain. You will also need extra liquid to finish the sauce.

The process of straining the pulp from the skin and seeds is not necessary; Laura doesn't do it in her recipe. I've added this step because I find it's worth the effort to ensure a smooth sauce for myself and clients.

> **Gluten Free Option:**
> Use 1 T arrowroot mixed with 4 T cold water in place of flour.
>
> **Vegan Option:**
> use veggie stock in place of chicken stock.

To Finish the Sauce
3 T olive oil
5 cloves garlic - minced
3 T flour
1 tsp allspice
1 T oregano
1 T ground cumin
1 tsp black pepper
2 tsp kosher salt

Saute garlic in olive oil, add flour to make a roux, cook - stirring constantly for 5 minutes. Slowly whisk in cooking liquid until the roux is thinned. Add the pureed, strained red chiles and the rest of the cooking liquid, along with the spices and cook until slightly thickened.

If you are doing this gluten free - sauté garlic in olive oil. Add the strained red chile peppers, cooking liquid, and spices. Add 1 T arrowroot mixed with 4 T cold water. Cook until slightly thickened.

Guacamole
With Garlic & Lemon Juice

GF, DF & VG

I like my guacamole simple. You can add chopped green onions, loosely chopped cilantro and minced jalapenos if you prefer more ingredients. My Latina friends in Los Angeles add chopped tomatoes as well.

Serves 6

6 ripe avocados
1 to 2 lemons juiced - to taste
3 cloves garlic - minced
S & P

Cut the avocados in half and remove the pit. Using a spoon, scoop the flesh out of the skin and into a bowl. With a fork or a pastry knife, mash the avacado till smooth. Add the minced garlic, lemon juice and salt to taste. I like lemon. If you are not a big fan, start with one lemon.

Enchilada Sauce
With Vegetarian Enchiladas

✻ GF

Enough sauce for 1 (9x13) casserole pan

4 cloves garlic - minced
4 T olive oil
¾ C chili powder (my fave online at El Potrero Trading Post)
2 tsp cumin
2 tsp oregano
1 T arrowroot
4 C chicken stock (or veggie stock if VG)

Sauté garlic in olive oil. Add the spice mix, whisk in veggie or chicken stock. Simmer until thickened, about 5 minutes.

Enchiladas - *serves 12*

4 chicken breasts - cubed
1 pkg corn tortillas (30 pk)
3 C enchilada sauce (above)
1 bunch green onions - chopped
1 bunch kale - stemmed, thinly sliced
1 bunch cilantro - stemmed, chopped
½ tsp cumin & ½ tsp oregano, S & P
2 C corn - fresh Olathe® corn kernels or frozen corn kernels
2 C pinto beans - cooked (pg. 51)
2 C feta cheese - crumbled
1 (6 oz)can sliced black olives
1C grated Monterey jack cheese - to top
1 (6 oz) can whole black olives - to top

Vegan Option:
Omit chicken and cheese. For filling use 2, 8 oz tofutti cream cheese:
Mix with 2 tsp chili powder, ½ tsp garlic powder, ½ tsp onion powder ½ tsp salt. Use in place of feta cheese. Top with vegan hard cheese.

Cow Dairy Free Option:
Use goat feta for the filling and a hard goat gouda for topping.

Preheat oven to 350°. Sauté chicken breast in olive oil until browned, deglaze with 2 T tequila, set aside. Sauté onions in 2 T olive oil, add kale, cumin, oregano and corn. When kale is wilted add the rest of the ingredients. Remove from heat. Lightly oil a 9 x 13 pan. Add 1 C Enchilada Sauce. In a separate bowl, dip one corn tortilla at a time in enchilada sauce. Add chicken, ⅓ C filling, roll tortilla and lay in pan. Continue until the pan is full. Cover with enchilada sauce, and top with grated Monterey jack cheese and black olives. Bake for 30 minutes covered with foil and 30 minutes uncovered until brown.

Mac N' Cheese
With Goat Cheese Option

Serves 8

1 lb penne pasta
1 C Gruyére cheese - grated
1 C sharp cheddar cheese - grated
1 C Parmesan cheese - finely grated
1 tsp kosher salt
¼ tsp fresh cracked pepper
4 tsp butter
4 tsp flour
1½ C heavy cream or milk
1½ C fresh bread crumbs (about ½ baguette)

Preheat oven to 400°.

Bread Crumbs -
In a food processor, add baguette pieces and pulse into small crumbs. Spread fresh bread crumbs onto a sheet pan, season with S & P. Bake about 10 minutes until golden brown. Cool. Add ½ C Parmesan cheese to cooled bread crumbs. This will be your topping.

Pasta -
Boil penne pasta in salted water. Strain.

Roux -
Melt butter in a small sauce pan, add flour and whisk. Cook and stir on medium heat for 2 minutes to cook the flour. Add cream or milk and whisk until thickened, about 2 minutes. Set aside.

Set aside ½ C of Parmesan cheese for bread crumb topping. Put the rest in a bowl along with the Gruyére and sharp cheddar cheese. Add hot cooked pasta to cheese mix, then add roux.

Pour pasta/cheese mix into a greased 8" x 8" baking dish. Top with bread crumb mixture and bake for about 10 to 20 minutes until topping is golden brown.

Gluten Free Option:
Use gluten free penne pasta. Tinkyada® Brown Rice Pasta or La Venezaine® Pasta, are good choices. Add 2 T Arrowroot in place of flour. Also use gluten free dried bread crumbs, mix with Parmesan cheese.

For Cow Dairy Free Option:
Replace the cow cheese ingredients, with 2 C goat gouda and 1 C soft goat brie.

For the roux, use 4 tsp coconut oil (pg. 10) & 1½ C coconut milk in the carton (pg. 10). Don't use cheese in the bread crumb mix.

Casein Allergies -
Casein is a protein in milk. Most people who have casein allergies cannot tolerate milk or dairy of any kind. But some, can handle the casein of goat cheese. The harder the cheese, the better it's tolerated.

Penne à la Vodka
With Prosciutto

I've startled myself and clients with this one. Use extreme caution when adding the vodka; it will shoot up a surprising flame if you aren't careful.

Serves 8
2 lbs penne pasta
½-1 lb prosciutto - thinly sliced
2 T olive oil
4-5 garlic cloves - minced
1 (6 oz) can tomato paste
½ C vodka
1 C white wine
3-4 C heavy cream
1 C Parmesan cheese - fine grated
S & P
To finish:
2 pints cherry tomatoes - slice in half
1 (.66 oz) pkg basil - chiffonade
Parmesan or Manchego cheese to top - shaved

Dairy Free Option: Use coconut milk in the carton and omit the heavy cream and Parmesan cheese.

Gluten Free Option: Use gluten free pasta. Tinkyada® Brown Rice Pasta or La Venezaine® Pasta, both are good choices. The first is made from brown rice, the second is made from corn.

Cook penne pasta in salted water until al dente. Strain.

Sauté prosciutto in olive oil. Add garlic and cook for 1 minute.
Add tomato paste and mix. Turn off heat and deglaze with vodka, BE CAREFUL OF FLAME. If it ignites, take the pan away from stove. Once the flame dies down you can put back on heat.
Reduce vodka down until thick. Add wine, reduce 5 minutes more. Add heavy cream and cook 10 minutes more.

When pasta is cooked, strain and add sauce, grated Parmesan and tomatoes. Top with basil and shaved Parmesan.

Tofu Stuffed Pasta Shells
With Primavera Sauce

❄ DF

Makes 2 pans (1 pan serves 8)

2 lbs large pasta shells - cooked in salted water until al denté
2 lbs fresh spinach - wilted (add to a sauté pan with ¼ C boiling water, toss until wilted)
2 lbs Italian sausage - cooked and crumbled

Tofu (Ricotta) Cheese Mixture
1 C cashews
3-4 cloves garlic
2 T olive oil
2 lemons - zested and juiced
1 container extra firm tofu
1 8oz container Tofutti® Better Than Cream Cheese
2 tsp chile powder
¼ tsp onion powder
½ tsp salt

In Cuisinart® pulse cashews, garlic, olive oil and lemons. Drain and squeeze tofu to remove most of the liquid. Add tofu and remaining ingredients to Cuisinart®, mix well. Refrigerate over-night.

Primavera Sauce
1 onion - diced
4 cloves garlic - minced
6 carrots - small dice
2 zucchinis - quartered and sliced
2 eggplants - sliced, sweated and diced - (optional)
2 C button mushrooms - quartered
2 (28 oz) cans diced tomatoes
1 (28 oz) can tomato sauce
¼ C each, fresh basil and parsley - chopped

Sauté onion in 2 T olive oil until translucent. Add the rest of the veggies and sauté 10 minutes. Add diced tomatoes and tomato sauce, cook another 20 minutes. Add fresh basil, parsley, S & P to taste.

Preheat oven to 350°. Grease 9 x 13 baking dish. Add 2 C Primavera Sauce to pan. Stuff cooked pasta shells with a layer of wilted spinach, italian sausage and Tofu Cheese Mixture. Add to pan laying stuffed shells side by side with the opening down, until pan is full. Top with primavera sauce. If you can tollerate cassein, top with rice or soy motzerella cheese.

Bake for 45 minutes uncovered.

> **Gluten Free Lasagna Option:**
> Use gluten free lasagna pasta; boil until al dente, drain and layer. First, primavera sauce, then lasagna noodles, then cheese mixture, italian sausage and spinach. Repeat until your pan is full.

> **Vegan Option:**
> Omit Italian sausage.

> **To Sweat Eggplants -**
> Slice eggplants into ¼" slices and layer in a strainer. (Add kosher salt to both sides.) Add another layer and repeat. The salt will sweat the eggplants and remove the bitter juices. After 30 minutes, rinse well.

Spaghetti Carbonara
With Bacon or Panchetta

Serves 6
6 egg yokes
½ C heavy cream - room temperature
1¼ C Parmesan cheese - finely grate
9 oz spaghetti noodles
½ tsp kosher salt
11 oz pancetta or slab bacon - cut into matchsticks
3 cloves garlic - minced
¼ tsp crushed red pepper
1 T olive oil
½ tsp fresh ground black pepper

Gluten Free Option: Use gluten free pasta. Tinkyada® Brown Rice Pasta or La Venezaine® Pasta, both are good choices. The first is made from brown rice, the second is made from corn.

Mix eggs, and ¾ C Parmesan cheese. Set aside.

Bring a large pot of salted water to a boil (add ½ tsp kosher salt to water). Add pasta and cook for 8 to 10 minutes, until pasta is al denté. Strain.

At the same time: in a large skillet, sauté pancetta in olive oil until crispy. Add garlic, crushed red pepper and sauté one more minute. Add heavy cream and cook 2 minutes. Add the strained hot pasta to the pancetta mix, turn off heat and add egg and cheese mixture. Mix thoroughly. Garnish with fresh ground black pepper and the extra ½ C grated Parmesan cheese.

It's very important that the pasta/pancetta mix is hot when you add the egg mix - this will ensure the raw eggs are thoroughly cooked.

Cajun Blackening Seasoning Mix

GF, DF & VG

For Blackened Steak or Ahi

Makes enough to store in pint jar

Seasoning Mix:
4 T paprika
10 tsp kosher salt
4 tsp onion powder
4 tsp garlic powder
4 tsp cayenne
3 tsp white pepper
3 tsp black pepper
2 tsp thyme
2 tsp oregano

This stores well in an airtight container for at least 6 months.

Blackened Steak or Ahi   **GF**
2 ribeye steaks
or
2 (1-1½") ahi steaks
4 T butter
1-2 T Cajun Blackening Seasoning Mix

> **Dairy Free Option:**
> Use Earth Balance® in place of butter.

Coat steak or fish with melted or warm butter. Then generously coat with seasoning.

Turn fan on and heat cast iron skillet until very hot, about 5 minutes. Add steaks or fish. Blacken on each side for 3 to 5 minutes. (3 minutes for rare, 5 minutes for medium rare.) If your ahi is fresh sushi grade, you can sear for one minute on each side, it will be raw in the middle and seared on the outside. Don't eat raw fish, unless you know your sources and can verify it's sushi grade and safe to eat raw.

You MUST have a good fan or commercial hood to suck up the smoke. Or cook outside on your grill with a cast iron skillet. The smoke will set your smoke alarm off if you don't use your fan!

Collections from an Aspen Chef
Favorite recipes with options to accommodate your dietary preferences

Collections from an Aspen Chef
Favorite recipes with options to accommodate your dietary preferences

Canned Favorites:

Bread N' Butter Pickles	96
Laura's Peach Chutney	97
Peach Salsa	98
Canned Peaches	99
Sour Cherry Preserve	100
Peach Rhubarb Jam	101

GF = Gluten Free ～ DF = Dairy Free ～ VG = Vegan ～ ❄ = Freezes Well

Bread & Butter Pickles
With Sweet Onions

GF, DF & VG

I first tasted home canned bread and butter pickles when I was in Chicago visiting my former mother-in-law. This recipe is different than hers, but along the same lines. In place of pickling cucumbers, I have also used larger cucumbers from the garden that were harvested in the fall. The key to delicious, crunchy pickles is to use cucumbers fresh off the vine.

Makes about 6 pint jars
18 to 25 small pickling cucumbers or 8-9 larger cucumbers
2 sweet onions
½ C kosher salt

To keep the cucumbers crisp, this part of the recipe has to be done the day you get them from the market or pick from your garden. Choose the smaller, firmer cucumbers if possible.

Wash and scrub cucumbers. Slice about ½" thick. Then slice the onions ½" thick then into 4 quarters. Layer cucumbers, onions and salt in a bowl. Cover with cold water and add some ice. Cover and let soak overnight.

Syrup
3 C sugar
2 C cider vinegar
2 C white vinegar
2 tsp mustard seeds
1 tsp tumeric

Drain the cucumber/onion/salt mix and rinse. Bring syrup to a high rolling boil and add cucumbers and onions to syrup. Bring back to a boil then immediately remove from heat. While pickles are hot, add to hot sterilized jars and boil in a hot water bath for 30 minutes. (Don't use a pressure cooker to can pickles, they will come out mushy.)

> **To Sterilize Jars -**
> Wash jars well with soapy water and put into boiling water for 20 minutes. Put lids and rings into a separate sauce pan in water; bring to a boil then hold on a low simmer for 20 minutes before using. Check the canning guidelines for your altitude and jar size for canning times.

Laura's Peach Chutney
Southwest Meets India

❄ GF, DF & VG

Laura's Peach chutey is the best chutney I've tasted. She usually throws it together with a pinch here and a dab there. I watched her make it many times and wrote down an approximate recipe that I follow.

Makes about 8 pint jars
peaches - about ½ case
3 C cider vinegar
2 C sugar
1½ T fresh ginger - minced
4 cloves garlic minced
1 C red chile sauce (homemade pg 83) or 10 red chiles stemed and de- seeded

Spice Mix: 1 tsp each (except where noted) of:
    ground fenugreek
    ground cumin
    coriander seeds
    mustard seeds
    black pepper
    2 cinnamon sticks
    turmeric
    ½ tsp nutmeg
    ½ tsp kosher salt
    1 T chile powder
    2 bay leaves

Bring a 2 gallon stock pot full of water to boil. Cut an **X** on the top of each peach. Drop them into boiling water and remove when skin starts to peel (about 1 minute). Peel and pit.

Cut peeled and pitted peaches into small wedges. Add to a 2 gallon stock pot, it should be about ⅔ full. Add the rest of the ingredients and the spice mix. Cook for about 20 minutes. Add hot chutney to hot sterilized jars (see pg. 96) and boil in a hot water bath for 30 minutes. Follow canning guidelines for your altitude and jar size.

Peach Salsa
With a Southwestern Flair

❄ **GF, DF & VG**

Makes about 8 pint jars
12 peaches - peeled and pitted
7 Early Girl tomatoes or Roma tomatoes – seeded and diced
4 bunches green onions - chopped
6 cloves garlic - minced
1-2 chipotle peppers canned in adobo sauce - minced
3 jalapeno chiles - seeded, fine diced
½ C roasted green chiles - medium diced
2 bunches cilantro - stemmed and chopped
½ C fresh lime juice
¼ C champagne or cider vinegar
S & P

Bring a 2 gallon stock pot full of water to boil. Cut an **X** on the top of each peach. Drop them into boiling water and remove when skin starts to peel (about 1 minute).
Peel and pit.

Cut peaches into ½" dice. Place peaches and the rest of the ingredients in a 2 gallon stock pot. Heat to a boil then take off the heat. They are ready to can or freeze. If canning, add to sterilized jars (pg 96) and follow canning guidelines for your altitude and jar size. I usually can pint and quart jars in a hot water bath for 30 minutes at 8,000 feet. If freezing, add to freezer- safe containers, leaving ½" headspace or use a Seal-A-Meal® or FoodSaver® .

> **To Remove Tomato Seeds -**
> To remove tomato seeds use a sharp knife. Start at the top where the stem comes out and slice down the contour of the side to the bottom - slicing the flesh off of the sides of the tomato. This will leave the seed clump to discard. Dice the sliced tomato flesh.

Canned Paonia Peaches
Colorado Grown or your own Local Organic Peaches

GF, DF & VG

Makes about 8 quart jars
24 peaches - peeled and pitted
2 lemons juiced or substitute ascorbic acid (follow directions on label)
canning jars - quarts and pints

Peaches
Bring a 2 gallon stock pot full of water to boil. Cut an **X** on the top of each peach. Drop them into boiling water and remove when skin starts to peel (about 1 minute).
Peel and pit.

Cut peaches in half and put into a large bowl with either lemon juice or water and ascorbic acid. You can find ascorbic acid in the canning section of the grocery store. Read the label for amounts to use. This will stop the browning.

Syrup
8 C boiling water
2 C sugar

Boil water, add sugar. Keep the syrup at a simmer until you add it to the peach-filled canning jars.

Add the halved peaches to sterilized canning jars (pg 96), fill with syrup, leaving a ½" headspace. Boil in hot water bath for 30 minutes and follow canning guidelines for your altitude and jar size.

Sour Cherry Preserves
With Pie Cherries

GF, DF & VG

Makes about 7 half-pint jars
5 C pie cherries - pitted (either fresh or frozen, from your farmers market)
4½ C sugar
2 T lemon juice
1 (2 oz) pkg liquid pectin

Macerate cherries, sugar and lemon juice in the sauce pan you will be using. Let stand for 1 to 2 hours before heating. (This is to let the cherries soften and release liquid and meld with the sugar).

Place pan over medium heat until sugar is completely dissolved. Bring to a low boil for 10 minutes. Then bring to a high rolling boil and add liquid pectin. Continue boiling, stirring constantly for 1 minute. Remove from heat and let the mix cool for 5 minutes before placing in sterilized canning jars (pg 92). Follow canning guidelines for your altitude and jar size. I usually boil pint jars for 20 minutes and quart jars for 25 minutes, at 8,000 feet.

Most recipes call for 7 cups of sugar; because I use less sugar, the preserves come out syrupy instead of firm. If you want a firmer preserve, use 7 cups of sugar.

Peach Rhubarb Jam
From the Garden

GF, DF & VG

Makes about 10 half-pint jars
5 C rhubarb - large dice
5 C peaches - pealed, pitted and medium dice (about 6 or 7 peaches)
8 C sugar
1 lemon - juiced
2 (2 oz) pkg pouches liquid pectin

Peaches
Bring a 2 gallon stock pot full of water to boil. Cut an **X** on the top of each peach. Drop them into boiling water and remove when skin starts to peel (about 1 minute).
Peel and pit.

Jam
Add rhubarb and peaches to a 2 gallon stock pot, then add sugar and lemon. Bring to a boil and keep on medium heat for about 10 minutes. Then bring to a high rolling boil and add liquid pectin. Boil, stirring constantly for 1 minute. Take off heat and let cool for 5 minutes before placing in sterilized canning jars (pg. 96). This will help keep the fruit from floating. Leave a ½" headspace in jar.

Rhubarb -
Cut fresh rhubarb at the base of the stalk and remove the leaves - the leaves are poisionous! Wash the stalks and cut into one inch pieces. Put 5 C portions in the freezer and bring out for pies or this yummy jam.

Follow canning guidelines for your altitude and jar size. I usually boil pint jars for 20 minutes and quart jars for 25 minutes, at 8,000 feet.

Most recipes would call for 14 cups of sugar; because I use less sugar, the jam comes out syrupy instead of firm. IF you want a firmer jam, use 14 cups of sugar.

Collections from an Aspen Chef
Favorite recipes with options to accommodate your dietary preferences

Poultry:

Oven Roasted Turkey w/Will's Brine	104
Indian Curry w/Chicken	105
Thai Red Curry Sauce w/Chicken	106
Chicken Under a Brick w/Herbed Pesto	107
Coq au Vin	108
Hillbilly Chicken	109
Fried chicken	110

Lamb:

Butterflied Leg of Lamb	111
Asian Glazed Lamb Chops	112
Herb Crusted Rack of Lamb	113

Beef:

Linda's Dry Beef Curry	114
Steak au Poivre	115

Collections from an Aspen Chef
Favorite recipes with options to accommodate your dietary preferences

Beef Continued:

Beef Tenderloin w/Port Wine Reduction	116
Filet Mignon w/Pomegranate Reduction	117
Prime Rib Au Jus	118
Beef Stroganoff	119

Pork:

Baby Back Ribs w/Hoison Glaze	120
Herb Crusted Pork Tenderloin	121
Cuban Braised Pork Butt or Shoulder	122

Fish:

Ruby Red Trout w/Tomatoes & Dill	123
Chipotle Glazed Salmon	124
Parchment Wrapped Halibut	125

GF = Gluten Free ~ DF = Dairy Free ~ VG = Vegan ~ ❄ = Freezes Well

Oven Roasted Turkey with Will's Brine DF
And Gravy from the Drippings

Will's brine will render your turkey moist and delicious with a dark, rich brown skin. Will is a friend who worked at the specialty store where I shopped for my clients. He loves to cook and share his gift.

Serves 10

1 (18 to 26 lb) turkey
1 turkey size Reynolds® Oven Baking Bag
1 bottle of inexpensive champagne
2 tsp Tony Chachere's® Creole Seasoning

One day before roasting, follow instructions for Will's Brine (below). After marinating, take turkey out of brine and pat it dry. Season skin with cajun seasoning. Place in a Reynolds® Oven Baking Bag and bake at 350° for 3-5 hours, until internal temperature reaches 165°-170°. I like to add most of a bottle champagne around the outside of bird inside the Reynolds bag. This makes a great gravy. Be sure to poke 5-6 holes in the top of the bag with a knife before baking, this will release steam pressure.

> **Gluten Free Option:**
> For the brine, use a GF beer in place of the stout.
>
> For the gravy - replace flour with 2 T arrowroot dissolved into ¼ C cold water, whisk with a fork to mix. Add to the onion and turkey drippings. Whisk until incorporated.

Will's Brine

1 (18 to 26 lb) bird
water - enough to cover bird and the other ingredients
1 C sugar
1 C kosher salt
2 stout beers like Guinness®
⅔ C dark molasses
1 head garlic - cloves, peeled and cut in halves (I use 5 cloves instead of a whole head)
4 sprigs fresh sage
4 sprigs fresh thyme

Dissolve the salt and sugar in approximately 8 cups of very hot tap water. Add the remaining brine ingredients. If needed, add ice cubes to the brine mix to chill it. Place the bird in the brine mix. Then add enough cold water to cover the bird. Use either a 5 gallon stock pot that you can put into a cold garage or refrigerator, or a cooler lined with a BPA free, food safe plastic bag - remove the air and tie bag off. Then place ice over that. It should be in kept at about 40°. Marinate overnight, at least 12-14 hrs.

Gravy

Sauté 1 finely chopped onion in 2 T olive oil until translucent. Add 3 minced garlic cloves and sauté one more minute. Sprinkle ¼ C flour over the onions and stir well. Slowly add the turkey drippings, whisking constantly to incorporate the flour. If you need more liquid, add some chicken stock. Keep warm while you carve the bird. Reserve ¾ C of drippings into a roasting pan to hold carved meat and keep moist.

To Carve the Bird - Cut the breast meat off bones in one piece and place on cutting board. Thinly slice across the breast. Keep the breast intact and put back in pan with drippings. Remove legs and wings. Carve thighs and legs into manageable pieces. Put into pan drippings. Cover and keep warm until you serve.

Indian Curry with Chicken
With Coconut Milk

❄ **GF & DF**

Serves 10

3 T olive oil
1 large onion - medium diced
6 lg garlic cloves - minced
8 carrots - peeled and sliced on the diagonal
1 bunch celery - sliced on the diagonal
2 C mushrooms - cleaned and sliced
1 bunch kale - stemmed and thinly sliced
2 zucchinis - quartered and sliced
2 red peppers - seeded, sliced on the diagonal
2 T ginger - minced
4 jalapenos - fine dice
4 T curry powder
1 T cumin
½ tsp cayenne
1 (8 oz) can sliced water chestnuts - julienne
4 C chicken stock
2 (28 oz) can diced tomatoes drained
4 (13.66 oz) cans coconut milk, unsweetened
2 C coconut milk in the carton
2 T brown sugar

Vegan Option: Omit the chicken or shrimp. Use vegetable stock in place of chicken stock. Omit the yogurt from the toppings. Or you can use a plain coconut yogurt to substitue dairy yogurt in your toppings.

Sauté onion, carrot and celery in olive oil for 5 minutes. Add the rest of the veggies, spices, stock, tomatoes, coconut milks and brown sugar. Cook until veggies are tender. Can be made up to 2 days ahead.

Add the following ingredients to low-rolling-boiling soup and cook until meat is done.

4 lbs chicken breasts - sliced into ⅛-¼" strips on the diagonal
2 lbs shrimp – (optional) - peeled and deveined
¼ C cilantro - chopped, to finish curry
Serve on top of rice (pg. 106) with condiment sides.

Condiment Sides
shredded coconut
cilantro - chopped
green onions - sliced on the diagonal
yellow raisins
peach chutney (pg. 97)
Fuji apples - small dice, marinate in lemon juice
cashews
plain yogurt

Thai Red Curry
With Chicken & Jasmine Rice

Red Chili Paste

❄ GF, DF & VG

15 to 20 Thai bird chili peppers or chili de árbol peppers
1 T coriander seeds (or 3 tsp ground)
1 T cumin seeds (or 3 tsp ground)
1 tsp black pepper
1 tsp kosher salt
5 Fresno chiles (red jalapenos-seasonal) - seeded, remove ribs
3 serrano peppers - seeded, remove ribs
2 stalks lemongrass (use white and 2 inches of green) - small chop
4 garlic cloves - peeled
2 shallots - large dice
1 bunch cilantro – stems and leaves
2 T peeled galangal root - minced (or 1½ T ground)
2 T fresh ginger root - minced
2 limes - zested and juiced
2 T brown sugar

Remove stems and seeds of Thai bird or chili de árbol peppers and soak in warm water for 20 minutes. Add to a food processor. Toast cumin and coriander seeds. Grind with a mortar and pestle. Add to food processor. Then add the rest of the ingredients, pulse until minced. Add 2-4 tablespoons of water to make a paste. At this point it freezes well. Use or freeze ⅓ C portions.

Thai Red Curry with Red Chili Paste (above) - *Serves 10*

GF & DF

2 red potatoes - medium dice
3 carrots - sliced
⅓ C Thai red chili paste (above)
¼ C brown sugar
¼ C fish sauce
2 (13.66 oz) cans coconut milk - unsweetened
4 chicken breasts - sliced ⅛-¼" on the diagonal
2 C mushrooms - sliced or quartered
1 red pepper - seeded and julienne sliced
2 zucchinis - quartered lengthwise and ¼" slice
1 bunch kale - stemmed and thinly sliced

Vegan Option: Omit the chicken and add more veggies.

Before starting the curry, parboil the potatoes and carrots until fork tender. Drain and set aside. Take ⅓ cup of red chili paste and saute in 2 T olive oil for about 2 minutes. Open cans of coconut milk, scoop out the solid portion and add to the chili paste. Cook until it bubbles and separates. Then add brown sugar, fish sauce and the remaining coconut milk and mix well. Add mushrooms, red pepper, kale and zucchini. Cook 5-8 minutes. Then add chicken and cook 5-8 minutes longer, until chicken is cooked. Add potatoes and carrots. Serve on Jasmine rice.

Jasmine Rice-
2 C Jasmine rice uncooked and 4 C water

Bring water to a boil. Add jasmine rice. Cover and simmer for 20 minutes. Fluff with a fork.

Chicken Under a Brick
With Herbed Pesto

GF & DF

This is a fun dish, but you need to be careful. I've sent flames up on the stove top while flipping the bird from skin side to bone side. It gave my clients a fright. Take care to turn off the heat before you flip over the bird.

Serves 6 to 10
Preheat oven to 375°
2 to 4 roaster chickens, organic and hormone-free
2 to 4 T olive oil
Tony Chachere's® Creole Seasoning

Cut the spine out of the chicken with kitchen shears. Grab each side of the chicken, bend the breast together to crack the bones and flatten out. (This will eliminate the use of a brick to flatten out the chicken.)

Heat olive oil in cast iron or non-stick skillet. Add chicken, skin side down. Sear skin-side down 10 to 15 minutes until golden crispy brown. (I cover the pan with foil to keep the mess down). IMPORTANT: make sure you turn heat off before you flip over the bird to bone side down - it could flame up! Apply coating of pesto mix under wings and between thighs, not on the breast or thigh skin. It will burn if you add to the crispy skin while baking. You can either leave in your oven-safe skillet or place in a baking pan and put into a 375° oven for 1 hour.

Also good without Herbed Pesto Mix. Instead sprinkle skin with cajun seasoning.

Herbed Pesto Mix

GF, DF & VG

1 lemon – zest and juice
3 T olive oil
1 (.66oz) pkg fresh thyme - strip the leaves off stem
1 bunch parsley - stems removed

Pulse all of the ingredients in a food processor into a paste.

Coq au Vin
With Chicken Thighs

DF

My dear friend Barbara from Boulder, Colorado, made Coq au Vin for dinner while I was visiting. It was so delicious I came up with my own version and started sharing it with my Aspen clients.

Serves 10

8 chicken thighs w/skin & bone
3 T olive oil
1 (750 ml) bottle red wine
½ onion- fine dice
2 stalks celery - fine dice
½ lb mushrooms - cleaned and sliced
2 carrots - fine dice
3 cloves garlic - minced
3 T tomato paste - heaping
1 C beef broth (or chicken stock)
1 bay leaf
1½ tsp dried thyme or 3 tsp fresh
¼ C flour
S & P
½ bag frozen peas - to finish
1 bag Egg Noodles

Gluten Free Option:
In place of flour use 1 T arrowroot dissolved into ¼ C cold water, whisk with a fork and mix thoroughly.

In place of egg noodles use gluten free noodles.

Deglazing -
A cooking technique using liquid to remove and dissolve browned food residue from the bottom of a pan. The browned bits are called *fond* (french for "base" or "foundation"); and is used to create delicious sauces, soups and gravies.

Sauté chicken thighs in olive oil, skin side down. Cook until skin is crispy and brown. Flip chicken and remove the skin, then brown on skinless side. Transfer to a Dutch oven or 2 gallon oven safe stock pot. You may need to do this in batches, depending on the size of your pan. Deglaze the pan between batches with some of the wine, transfer to the Dutch oven. Add all of the sauteéd chicken thighs and deglazed *fond* (see side bar) to the Dutch oven. Cover and cook on low for 8 to10 minutes.

In a separate pan sauté the onions, celery, mushrooms and carrots until the onions are translucent and the mushrooms are browned. Add garlic and cook 1 more minute. Add vegetables, garlic, and remaining wine to the Dutch oven along with the rest of the ingredients, except the flour. Cook uncovered for 25 minutes.

Remove the chicken. Place a laddle full of hot liquid to a bowl and add the flour, whisk until no lumps are visible. Return to Dutch oven and reduce until thickened. Then add the chicken back to the Dutch oven. (This can be done earlier in the day, reheat before serving.)

Before serving, add the frozen peas, heat until warm. Serve over al denté Egg Noodles.

Hillbilly Chicken
Cooked Sitting on a Can of Wine, Bourbon & Chicken Stock

GF & DF

This is a favorite for most of my clients, especially Lee and Tom. It's easy, looks really interesting, and tastes amazing! Although there is nothing hillbilly about it, I got the name from "Beer butt chicken" a southern favorite usually done on a grill with a can of beer up the cavity. I've refined it with a combo of wine, whiskey and chicken stock.

Serves 3-4
1 (3 to 5 lb) organic, hormone-free roaster chicken
1 tsp Tony Chachere's® Creole Seasoning
1 empty soda or beer can - washed out
1 T Jack Daniels whiskey
3 T white wine
½ C chicken stock
1 tsp arrowroot mixed with ½ C cold water

Gluten Free Option: Use a gluten free alcohol like brandy, make sure it's not flavored.

Preheat oven to 350°. Rinse the chicken under cold water and pat dry. Sprinkle with cajun seasoning. Pour whiskey, wine and chicken stock into the opening of the empty beer or soda can. Sit the bird on top of the can and insert the can into the cavity. Prop the legs in front of the can for stability, so the can and the legs make a tripod. Set the bird on a sheet pan with a lip to catch the juices from the cooking bird.

Roast the chicken for 1½ - 2 hours, until the internal temperature reaches 165°-170°. First carve the spine off on both sides to butterfly the chicken. Cut the breast meat away from the ribs. Cut thigh away from the leg. Don't stack or place chicken skin side down or the skin will get soggy.

Gluten Free WARNING: Some experts say that the distillation process removes harmful gluten proteins from alcohol. Some experts advise using only alcohol made from non-gluten grain sources. Use your own judgement if you are allergic to gluten. Some alcohol distilleries might add caramel color which can contain gluten.

Remove the can, add the liquid to a sauce pan, along with the pan drippings. Add arrowroot to water and mix with a fork. Add to the sauce. Reduce until thick and serve as a gravy (5-10 minutes).

Platter and serve with the gravy on the side.

Collections from an Aspen Chef ~ Cindy Rogers

Fried Chicken
With Dairy Free Option

Serves 6

2 whole chickens, organic and hormone-free - cut into pieces
1 C buttermilk
2 eggs - beaten
2 tsp dried thyme
2 tsp kosher salt
1 tsp fresh cracked pepper
1 C flour
½ C cornmeal
1 C Special K® cereal or corn flakes
canola oil

Cut chicken into pieces. Wash and pat dry.
In a big bowl mix buttermilk, eggs, thyme. Add chicken and soak overnight if possible - or at least 3 hours.

Mix cornmeal and flour, add cereal, salt, and pepper. Heavily coat each piece with the dry mix and put on a drying rack for half and hour to 1 hour.

Preheat oven to 350°.
Fry chicken in canola oil. If you have a fryer use it. If not add 2" of canola oil in a dutch oven and fry chicken on one side, then flip. Don't crowd the pot. Leave some space between chicken pieces. Fry until golden brown and set on an oven-safe cooling or baking rack. Before serving place the cooling rack on a sheet pan and bake in oven for 30 - 45 minutes until chicken is fully cooked (165°-170°). Use a meat thermometer, or cut a breast in half to see if the meat is cooked and its juices run clear. This is great for a dinner party, you can get the recipe prepped ahead and just pop it in the oven before serving. I have prepped this 4 hours before a dinner party and no one could tell the difference.

Gluten Free Option:
Use ¾ C rice flour and ¼ C potato starch, in place of flour use a GF flake cereal with rice or corn (check the label).

Dairy Free Option:
Use coconut milk in place of buttermilk.

Cooling or Baking Racks -
Oven-safe racks made of metal used for cooling or baking. They are elevated to allow airflow to either cool baked goods or keep meat or whatever you are baking out of juices.

Butterflied Leg of Lamb
With Mint, Oregano and Lemon Pesto

GF & DF

Serves 6
1 leg of lamb - butterflied

Marinade Paste
2 (.66 oz) pkgs oregano or 2 C fresh from the garden
6 cloves of garlic
2 lemons - zest and juice
1 C high quality extra virgin olive oil
1 tsp kosher salt
½ tsp fresh ground pepper

Have your butcher butterfly and debone a leg of lamb. Otherwise, with a very sharp knife, trim fat off leg and find a seam between muscles. Work your knife in between the muscles and carve toward the bone and trim the bone out.
This will butterfly your leg of lamb. I like to trim off all the fat and silverskin. This will leave you with about 4 segments of the leg when you're done.

In a food processor, add oregano, garlic, zest and juice of lemons (first peel zest off lemon with a potato peeler, slice in half and juice the lemon), salt and pepper - drizzle in olive oil, enough to make a paste.

Rub lamb with olive oil then coat with herb paste. Marinate for at least 8 hours.
Heat the grill to high and put lamb on long enough to make a good grill mark on each side (about 2 minutes per side). Then, turn the grill to medium heat and cook until meat temperature registers 125° for rare and 135° for medium rare, about 20 - 25 minutes.

Slice against grain in ¼" slices and serve with mint sauce.

Mint/Oregano Pesto

GF, DF & VG

3 (.66 oz) pkgs mint - stemmed
1 (.66 oz) pkg oregano - stemmed
2 garlic cloves - peeled
1 tsp honey
2 tsp Dijon mustard
3 T rice wine vinegar
⅓ C olive oil
S & P

Add mint, oregano and garlic to a food processor. Pulse until finely chopped. Add honey, Dijon, vinegar, S & P. Pulse until mixed. Slowly drizzle olive oil through the top hole of your food processor and emulsify.

Asian Glazed Lamb Chops
With Hoisin Sauce

GF & DF

Serves 6
12 lamb chops or 3 racks Lamb

Marinade & Sauce
⅔ C hoisin sauce (check lable for GF)
½ C sugar
½ C honey
½ C chili garlic sauce
¼ C rice wine vinegar
2 T garlic - minced
2 T ginger - minced
2 T low sodium tamari sauce
2 T toasted sesame oil

If using chops, no extra work is necessary. If using racks, I like to French trim the rack and cut into 2 rib/riblets sections. (French trim instructions on pg 113).

Mix the marinade ingredients and marinate lamb for 1 hour. Heat the grill to high. Place lamb on grill long enough to make a good grill mark on each side - about 2 minutes per side. Turn the grill to medium heat and cook until meat temperature registers 125° for rare and 135° for medium rare. About 5 minutes total for rare - 8 minutes for medium rare.

Save the marinade and reduce the sauce until thick. Serve over the chops or riblets.

Always use a sharp knife and cut through one of your pieces of meat to determine doneness. You want your meat pinkish red, but not blue (blue is still raw).

Herbed Crusted Rack of Lamb
With Shallots & Thyme

DF

Serves 4

2 racks of lamb - french trimmed
3 T Dijon mustard
3 T olive oil
6 large shallots - chopped (about 1 C)
6 T balsamic vinegar
1 C fresh bread crumbs
3 T fresh thyme - chopped

Herb Crust
Sauté shallots until translucent. Add vinegar and thyme, reduce down until syrupy. Add bread crumbs and mix until combined and moist.

Preheat oven to 375°. Coat lamb meat with Dijon (this helps the crust stick to the meat). Then coat with herb crust and bake at 375° for 25 minutes, until temperature registers 125° for rare and 135° for medium rare.

To French Trim Rack of Lamb
I like to remove all the fat and silverskin from the rack. Using your fingers, get under the first layer of fat, pull it up and carve it off with a very sharp knife. This will make the second layer of fat and silverskin easier to remove - proceed with your knife. Run a sharp knife down each side of the rib bones and cut off the fat at the sides and base where the ribs connect to the meat. Carve the fat off in a U shape - down one rib, across the fat connecting the meat, then back up the next rib.

Mint Sauce

GF, DF & VG

3 C fresh mint
1 cloves garlic
2 tsp Dijon mustard
2 tsp honey
¼ C olive oil
¼ C rice wine vinegar
S & P

Add mint and garlic to a food processor. Pulse until fine chopped. Add honey, Dijon, vinegar, S & P. Pulse until mixed. Slowly drizzle olive oil through the top hole of your food processor and emulsify.

Gluten Free Option:
Omit the bread crumbs and reduce sauce until it's syrupy. Cool and place on top of the Dijon layer to coat the lamb making a GF herb crust.

Silverskin -
A white and silvery connective tissue surrounding various muscles in animals. It does not break down in cooking and is extremely tough and chewy. It is best to remove before cooking.

Linda's Dry Beef Curry
A Dry Rub for Tenderloin or Sirloin

GF & DF

Linda is a friend of mine who usually doesn't have a lot of time to cook, between training for triathalon and ironman competions and working as a massage therapist for some of Aspens' finest athletes. When she does find the time...it's delicious!

Serves 6

2 lbs sirloin or beef tenderloin - sliced thin against the grain
½ C brown sugar
¾ C canola oil
3 T of dry rub mix (below)

Mix the brown sugar, ¼ C canola oil and dry rub mixture in a medium size bowl. Add the beef and coat well. Let beef marinate at least one hour. Heat the remaining canola oil in a heavy cast iron skillet. Add the beef to the hot oil, making sure not to crowd the meat in the pan. Cook for 1 minute and flip. Take out and drain onto paper towels. You can hold in a 200° oven or cover with foil until it's all cooked and ready to serve. Serve with Jasmine rice, below. Also good as a side to Red Thai curry pg. 106.

Dry Rub Ingredients:

GF, DF & VG

2 T curry powder
2 tsp cumin - ground
1 tsp coriander - ground
¾ tsp cardamom - ground
½ tsp paprika - ground
⅛ tsp cinnamon - ground
1 tsp kosher salt
½ tsp black pepper
½ tsp fenugreek - ground (optional)
½ tsp lemongrass - ground (optional)
¼ tsp white pepper

I like to quadruple the dry rub recipe and store it for future use. This will hold for at least a year in an air-tight container or jar, out of the sun and heat.

Jasmine Rice - *Serves 6*

GF, DF & VG

1 C jasmine rice
2 C water

Bring water to a boil. Add jasmine rice. Cover and simmer for 20 minutes. Fluff with a fork. This is a 2 part water to 1 part rice recipe. You can adjust the amounts as needed.

Steak au Poivre
With Green Peppercorn Sauce

GF

Serves 6 to 8
3 lbs sirloin steak
3 T butter

Green Peppercorn Sauce
2 shallots – chopped
3 T port
¼ C Cognac
1 C veal stock or glaze
3 T green peppercorns
S & P
1 C heavy cream
red wine vinegar – few drops

> **Dairy Free Option:**
> Use olive oil in place of the butter and So Delicious® coconut milk in place of the heavy cream.
>
> **Veal Stock Substitute:**
> In place of the veal stock you can use a mix of half chicken stock and half beef stock.

Preheat oven to 350°.
Sear both sides of the sirloin in the butter until brown (about 5 minutes per side), transfer to a sheet pan and cook in the oven for another 10-15 minutes or until the temperature reads 125° for rare, medium rare is 130°. Or you can sear meat and finish on the grill on medium heat.

In the same pan add chopped shallots, add more butter if needed for sautéing. Sauté until translucent. Add port and cognac to deglaze, then reduce until syrupy. Add the veal glaze and green peppercorns, cook 5 minutes. Add the heavy cream and cook another 5 minutes. Finish the sauce with a few drops of red wine vinegar.

Serve over sliced sirloin.

Grilled Beef Tenderloin
With Port Wine Reduction Sauce

GF & DF

Serves 6 to 8

1 whole beef tenderloin - trimmed
S & P

Have your butcher trim and tie your tenderloin. Sprinkle salt and fresh ground pepper onto the trimmed tenderloin.

For the Grill
Heat grill to high for 15 minutes, turn heat down to medium and place beef tenderloin on the grill. Sear on 4 sides to add grill marks. It should only take 25 - 30 minutes total to grill. Check the temperature; when it reaches 122° take off the grill and allow to rest under foil for about 10 minutes. It will continue cooking, temperatures should rise to 125° - 130°.

For the Oven
Rub beef tenderloin with butter or olive oil, sprinkle with salt and pepper. Bake in a preheated 350° oven for 25 – 30 minutes, until internal temperature reaches 122°. Take out of the oven and rest under foil for about 10 minutes. It will continue cooking and should rise to 125° - 130° for medium rare.

> **Substitutes:**
> In place of the port you can use Marsala or Maderia.
> In place of the veal stock you can use a mix of half chicken stock and half beef stock.

Port Wine Reduction Sauce - *can make a few days ahead, freezes well.*   ❄ **GF & DF**

2 shallots - minced
4 cloves garlic - minced
2 T olive oil
3 C port wine
4 C veal stock (check label if you need GF or DF)
1 T juniper berries
1 T fresh thyme
1 T fresh sage

Sauté shallots in olive oil, until translucent. Add garlic, then port, veal stock and the rest of the ingredients. Reduce by half on medium heat. This will take at least ½ hour.
You can also use Maderia or Marsala wine if you don't have any port.

Filet Mignon
With Pomegranate Reduction Sauce

GF & DF

Serves 8

8 beef filets - about 2 ½" thick
Heat grill to high and sear beef filets on both sides to get a good grill mark; about 5 minutes per side. Let rest 15 minutes. Rare is 125°, medium rare is 130°.

Pomegranate Reduction Sauce - *can make a few days ahead, freezes well.* ❄ GF & DF

3 T olive oil
1 medium yellow onion – diced
3 T minced - garlic
2 T whole black peppercorns
1 C port wine
6 C chicken stock
2 C pomegranate/acai juice blend - Naked Juice®
7 T pomegranate molasses (in specialty stores)
2 T light brown sugar
S & P

Sauté onions and garlic in olive oil. Add black peppercorns and cook 2 minutes. Add the port and reduce down until mostly evaporated. Add the rest of the ingredients and reduce by half, about 1½ hrs. Freeze what you don't use – it will keep at least 6 months in the freezer.

Serve pomegranate reduction sauce over filets. This is great with Baked Potato Fries pg. 76.

Prime Rib Au Jus
With Horsey Sauce

GF

Serves 6
1 (3 to 4 rib) standing rib roast (prime rib)
olive oil to coat meat
S & P
½ C red wine

Preheat oven to 450°.

Rub the prime-rib roast with olive oil, S & P. Sear in skillet on high, to brown on all sides. Remove meat and deglaze pan with ½ C red wine, reserve for au jus.

Put prime-rib roast into a roasting pan and bake at 450° degrees for 5 minutes. Turn heat down to 350° and continue baking for another 2½ hours until internal temperature reaches 122°. The temperature will rise 5 to 10 degrees while it rests.
Take out and let rest for 30 minutes. It can hold up to 1 hour. When the prime rib is done, take out of pan and set aside to rest. Use pan drippings for Au Jus (below). Trim and serve with hot Au Jus and Horsey sauce.

Au Jus
red wine reserved from deglaze above
2 C beef stock
pan drippings from the rib roast (above)

Add the pan drippings to the sauté pan in which you seared your prime rib. Include the deglaze wine and fond (see sidebar). Add 2 C beef stock. Heat and reduce for ½ hour. Serve hot over prime rib.

Horsey Sauce
2 to 3 T horseradish - prepared, not sauce
½ C sour cream
pinch of kosher salt

Add hot prepared horseradish to sour cream and kosher salt. (I like the Silver Springs® brand of horseradish, it's often in the refrigerated section by the fish).

Dairy Free Option: You can just serve plain prepared horseradish without mixing it with the sour cream. Make sure to read the label of the horseradish. Some brands have dairy added.

Deglazing - A cooking technique using liquid to remove and dissolve browned food residue from the bottom of a pan. The browned bits are called *fond* (french for "base" or "foundation"); and is used to create delicious sauces, soups and gravies.

Beef Stroganoff
With Wide Noodles or Pappardelle pasta

Serves 10

5 lbs beef tenderloin, or one whole loin
3 to 6 T canola oil
4 C button mushrooms - cleaned and quartered
2 yellow onions - diced
1 (750 ml) bottle red wine
5 T olive oil
3 T tomato paste
4 T dark brown sugar
4 T flour
2 C chicken stock
1 C beef stock
1 C sour cream
2 lbs pappardelle pasta or wide egg noodles
S & P

> **Dairy Free Option:**
> Omit the sour cream, it's still tasty without it.
>
> **Gluten Free Option:**
> Serve over gluten free pasta or rice. Use 2 T arrowroot mixed with 4 T water, in place of flour.
>
> **Silverskin -**
> A white and silvery connective tissue surrounding various muscles in animals. It does not break down in cooking and is extremely tough and chewy. It is best to remove before cooking.

Trim off silverskin and fat from beef tenderloin and cut into 1" pieces. Sauté batches in 2 T canola oil until brown. Deglaze pan with red wine between batches. Put sautéed meat and deglazed liquid in a bowl and set aside.

Sauté mushrooms in 3 T olive oil. The mushrooms will absorb all of the oil. Continue sautéing dry. They will release moisture as they sauté. Season with salt and pepper. Deglaze pan with red wine (about ¼ C) and cook until the mushrooms absorb the wine. Transfer to the bowl with beef and set aside.

Sauté onion in 2 T olive oil in a 2 gallon stock pot. Add tomato paste and brown sugar. Stir in flour and mix to incorporate. Add remaining wine, chicken and beef stock. Cook until thickened. Add the cooked beef, mushrooms and deglazing liquid.

Add 2 cups of the heated sauce to the sour cream in a separate bowl. Mix well, then add back to the sauce. This tempering process will keep the sour cream from curdling.

Serve over cooked wide egg noodles or pappardelle pasta if you can find it.

Asian Glazed Baby Back Ribs
With Hoisin Glaze

GF & DF

Serves 6

2 racks of pork ribs, St Louis style® (spare ribs trimmed to a rectangular-shaped rack)
S & P
large heavy duty foil

Preheat oven to 350°.
Pull a sheet of foil, long enough to double the length of a sheet pan. Place half of the foil on sheet pan. Lay both slabs of ribs on the foil, salt and pepper each side. Fold the extra foil over the meat and fold the edges inward to create a steam pouch. Bake at 350° for 2 hours.

Fold the top foil piece back and remove. Heavily coat the ribs with the hoisin glaze. Turn the oven off and let the ribs sit in the oven for 15 minutes with the oven door closed. Or at this point you can glaze ribs and grill on medium heat, (leave ribs on grill long enough to mark the meat with grill marks). Add more glaze and reheat in the oven before serving. Cut into individual ribs and serve with the remaining hoisin glaze on the side.

Hoisin Glaze

GF & DF

1 (7oz) jar hoisin sauce
¼ C honey
¼ C red wine vinegar
2 T grated fresh ginger
2-3 garlic cloves
1 T Chinese black vinegar or Worcestershire® sauce
1 tsp Thai red curry paste (see pg. 10)
1 T sesame oil
2 tsp curry powder

Fish Allergies - Worcestershire® sauce has anchovies. Omit and replace with tamari if you need to. Some Chinese black vinegar has gluten. Check the labels.

Place the ginger and garlic in a food processor. Add to a sauce pan with the rest of the ingredients. Heat until flavors have melded, about 5 minutes.

Cumin Crusted Pork Tenderloin

With Peach Chutney Sauce or Green Chile Sauce

GF & DF

Serves 6

2 pork tenderloin
2 T cumin seeds
Cajun Blackening Seasoning pg. 93 - enough to sprinkle on pork
¼ C olive oil

Coat pork tenderloin with olive oil and sprinkle liberally with Cajun Blackening Seasoning. Then coat with cumin seeds, pressing into meat.

Heat the grill to high. Place the pork tenderloin on the grill and reduce heat to medium. Turn meat 3 times, cooking a total of 25 minutes. Let rest for 5-10 minutes.

Serve with either-
Janette's green chili sauce (pg. 85).
Or
Laura's peach chutney (pg. 97).

Cuban Braised Pork
With Orange Juice & Oregano

GF & DF

Serves 10
1 (7 to 8 lb) pork shoulder bone-in
2 T olive oil to sear pork
4 cloves garlic
2 C fresh oregano (or 2 T dried)
2 T cumin ground
2 tsp Thai red curry paste (see pg. 10)
¼ C white vinegar or cider vinegar
3 C orange juice
1½ C chicken stock

In a Dutch oven or oven-safe 2 gallon stock pot, sear pork shoulder in olive oil – brown on all sides. Pulse the garlic, oregano, cumin, red chile paste and vinegar in a food processor. Add to Dutch oven along with chicken stock and orange juice.

Bake at 350° for 1½ hours. Flip pork and bake another 1½ hours. If the liquid gets really low add more chicken stock.

You can also do this in a slow cooker. Add all ingredients to the slow cooker and cook all day.

When done, pull meat apart with forks, add back to the cooking liquid. Serve with fries, rice or on a sandwich.

Ruby Red Trout
With Tomatoes & Dill

GF & DF

Serves 6

6 trout fillets - cleaned with skin on
6 Campari tomatoes - thinly sliced (or vine ripened tomatoes)
1 (.66 oz) pkg of dill or 6 sprigs of fresh dill
6 T lemon juice, about 2 lemons
6 T white wine
6 T olive oil
6 full sheet pieces of parchment paper
S & P

Preheat oven to 350°.
Lay out 6 sheets of parchment paper. Place 1 T olive oil in the center of each sheet. Add one trout fillet horizontally to each sheet and coat both sides in olive oil. Sprinkle S & P to season. Top with Campari tomato slices and one sprig of dill. Add 1 T each of white wine and lemon juice to the top of the fish.

With fish and parchment paper facing you horizontally, take the top and bottom sides of the parchment paper and hold up over fish. Fold together with half inch folds 2 to 3 times. Make sure you don't lose any of the liquid out of the ends. Take each end and twist shut, don't twist too tight or you will tear the parchment and have to rewrap it. (Think of the ends as a Tootsie Roll®).

Carefully cut off the excess paper at the ends so they can fit in the oven. Put 6 parchment-wrapped pieces on a sheet pan.

Bake for 10 minutes. Take each piece of parchment wrapped trout and open it onto individual plates. Don't forget to include the juice.

Chipotle Glazed Salmon
With Sour Cherry Preserves

GF & DF

Serves 8 to 10

1 side of wild caught salmon (about 2 lbs) - skin on
1 quart jar Sour Cherry Preserves pg. 100
2 to 4 chipotle peppers canned in adobo sauce - depending on preference for spicy
½ C ketchup
1 T toasted cumin seeds
1 lime – juiced
S & P

Toast cumin seeds, let cool. Add to a food processor with the Sour Cherry Preserves, chipotle peppers, ketchup, lime juice and S & P - pulse until chunky.

Cut salmon into 8 oz strips (or about 1½" wide). Place in a glass dish with skin side down. Generously add the cherry chipotle glaze to the top of the salmon and marinate for 1 to 2 hours.

Grill the salmon skin side down on high for 8 minutes. Flip and grill 2 minutes or long enough to put grill marks on it.

Heat and reduce sauce, serve on the salmon.

Parchment-Wrapped Halibut
With Veggie Medley

GF & DF

Serves 6

6 (8 oz) pieces of halibut - in season (fresh is better texture than frozen)
1 leek - cleaned, thin julienne sliced 4" long
1 red pepper - thin julienne sliced 4" long
1 zucchini - thin julienne sliced 4" long
1 (.66oz) pkg basil - chiffonade
12 T white wine (2 T per pouch)
6 T lemon juice
olive oil to coat fish
S & P
6 large pieces of parchment paper, big enough to cover a sheet pan.

Cleaning Leeks - Cut off root end. Cut green off 1 to 2" above white. I usually have a 5" segment left. Cut the trimmed leek in half lengthwise and run under cold water until the dirt is removed. Check in between layers to see that all the dirt is gone.

Preheat oven to 350°.
Chiffonade the basil. Stack leaves on top of each other. Roll them together, take a sharp knife and thinly slice across the roll.

Lay parchment sheets out on counter. Coat each piece of fish generously with olive oil. Place in the center of the parchment.
Add a small pile of the julienne veggies on top of the fish.

Add 2 T wine, 1 T lemon juice and about 1 T basil to each piece of fish. Add S & P to season.

With the fish and parchment paper facing you horizontally, take the top and bottom sides of the parchment paper and hold up over fish . Fold together into half inch folds 2 to 3 times. Make sure you don't lose any of the liquid out of the ends. Take each end and twist shut. Don't twist too tight or you will tear the parchment and have to rewrap it. (Think of the ends as a Tootsie Roll®). Carefully cut excess paper off at the ends so they can fit in the oven. Put 6 parchment-wrapped pieces onto a sheet pan.

Bake in a 350° oven for 20 to 25 minutes, depending on how thick the fish is. Open each piece of parchment-wrapped halibut onto individual plates. Don't forget to include the juice.

You can prep this dish up to 6 hours ahead of time. Hold in the refrigerator until ready to bake.

Collections from an Aspen Chef
Favorite recipes with options to accommodate your dietary preferences

Desserts:

Apple Tarte Tartin	128
Sour Cherry Pie	129
Granny's Apple Pie a la Mode	130
Paonia Peach Crisp	131
Lee's Raspberry Galette	132
Blueberry Cobbler	133
Vegan Chocolate Mousse	134
Coconut Mini Loaf Cakes	135
Chocolate Layered Mousse Cake	136
Chocolate Eruptions	137
Meringue Holiday Mushrooms	138
Bûche de Noël - Yule Log Cake	139

GF = Gluten Free ~ DF = Dairy Free ~ VG = Vegan ~ ❄ = Freezes Well

Collections from an Aspen Chef
Favorite recipes with options to accommodate your dietary preferences

Desserts:

Vegan Cheesecake	140
Grandmas Classic Cheesecake	141
Bananas Foster	142
Key Lime Pie w/Chocolate Wafer Crust	143
Mini Key Lime Frozen Treats	144
Candied Lemon Zest	145
Lemon Cake w/Lemon Curd & Seven Minute Icing	146
Lemon Lime Tart w/Kiwi & Berry Topping	147
Lemon Pudding Cakes	148
Poached Pears in a Pomegranate Açai Sauce	149
Chocolate Peanut Butter Torte	150
Raspberry Lemon Trifle	151

GF = Gluten Free ~ DF = Dairy Free ~ VG = Vegan ~ ❄ = Freezes Well

Apple Tarte Tartin
With Whipped Cream or A la Mode

Serves 8 - makes one Tarte

Pate Sucrée or Sweet Crust
1 stick (½ C) soft unsalted butter
⅓ C sugar
1 egg
2 C flour
2 pinches kosher salt
water - a little bit at a time to help it come together

Mix butter and sugar in a stand mixer. Add egg, then flour and salt. Add water until dough comes together. Form dough into a flat round disc and refrigerate for at least 1 hour. Roll out dough 1½" wider than an 8" round cake pan.

Tarte Tartin
6 T soft butter
⅓ C sugar
8 Granny Smith apples – peeled, cored and quartered

Preheat oven to 350°.
Heat an 8" round cake pan or an 8" cast-iron skillet on the stove-top. Add butter and melt. Add sugar and stir until dissolved. Then add quartered apples.
On low heat, caramelize sugar, about 15 – 20 minutes. Keep moving the pan around, stirring between the apple quarters, making sure not to burn the sauce or apples.

Take pan or skillet off the stove-top and add the rolled-out dough on top. Tuck the dough down inside the edges of the pan.

Bake at 350° until crust is well browned about 20 minutes.
Immediately invert onto a plate.

Serve with whipped cream or vanilla ice cream.

Sour Cherry Pie
With Cherries from the Farmers' Market

Basic Pie Crust - *makes 2 crusts (one for the base and one for the lattice)*
1½ C flour
¼ tsp baking powder
½ tsp kosher salt
¼ C butter
⅓ C lard
1 T apple cider vinegar
⅓ C ice cold water

Make at least 2 hours ahead, so it can go in the refrigerator or freezer. Dice butter and lard and put into the freezer for 10 minutes before starting crust. Add an ice cube to the water to chill it.

In mixer, add dry ingredients. While motor is running on low, add the butter and lard. Mix until incorporated and you have small crumbles. Then add vinegar and water until the dough holds together. Separate into two chunks, flatten dough into discs with your hands and wrap in plastic. Place in the refrigerator until needed. Or freeze for later.

Pie
5 C sour pie cherries - pitted
1-1½ C sugar
2 T orange juice concentrate
⅓ C tapioca flour (or corn starch)
⅛ tsp kosher salt
¼ tsp almond extract
1 egg yolk with 2 T heavy cream - for the egg wash.

Dairy Free & Vegan Oil Crust Option:
Use Olive Oil Crust pg. 179, using canola oil. Double the batch, so you will have enough for the base and lattice. Follow the instructions for the base of the pie. For the lattice, you want to be able to roll it out. If the dough is too crumbly add more coconut milk. (Use below intructions on this page for lattice).

Dairy Free & Vegan Option:
Use crust above and omit egg wash. Use water to pinch crust together.

Preheat oven to 425°.
If you have a cherry tree, fresh is the best. I usually use frozen pie cherries from the Aspen Farmers Market. Mix cherries, sugar and orange juice concentrate in a sauce pan, add the reamining ingredients, except egg wash. Heat on the stove to thicken juice into a syrup, then cool for 20 minutes. Roll out dough, place in pie dish. Add cherry filling to pie dish. Dot fruit with 2 T of butter. Roll out the remaining dough and use a ravioli cutter to cut 1" strips. Weave lattice strips on top of the pie. Leave about 2" of overhang and cut off the rest. Brush bottom dough edge with egg wash and pinch together the bottom and the top edges. Fold up and roll in, pinching the edges with your fingers. Coat the top of the pie with egg wash and bake.

Bake for 15 minutes at 425°. Reduce heat to 350° and bake 30–45 minutes, or until crust is golden brown and filling bubbles. Be sure to put a piece of foil under pie to catch spills as it bakes.

Granny's Apple Pie
A la Mode

Actually neither of my grandmothers cared about cooking. This recipe came from the granny of my childhood friend who loved to bake. She shared this recipe with me when I was 10 years old.

Basic Pie Crust - *makes 2 crusts (one for the base and one for the top)*

1½ c flour
¼ tsp baking powder
½ tsp kosher salt
¼ C butter
⅓ C lard
1 T apple cider vinegar
⅓ C ice cold water

Dairy Free Option:
Use Olive Oil Crust pg. 179, using canola oil. Add the Peach Crisp Crumble Mixture (pg. 131) to the top to make an apple betty pie.

Make at least 2 hours ahead, so it can go in the refrigerator or freezer. Dice butter and lard and place in the freezer for 10 minutes before starting crust. Add an ice cube to your water to chill it.
In mixer, add dry ingredients. While motor is running on low, add the butter and lard and mix until incorporated and you have small crumbles. Then add vinegar and water until the dough holds together. Separate into two chunks, flatten dough into discs with your hands and wrap in plastic. Place in the refrigerator until needed. Or freeze for later.

Apple Pie Filling

10 Granny Smith apples - peeled, cored and sliced in a food processor
1 lemon - juiced
¾ C sugar
¼ C flour
⅛ tsp kosher salt
1 tsp cinnamon
2 T butter
1 egg yolk with 2 T heavy cream - for the egg wash

Vegan Option:
Use crust above. Omit butter and egg wash from filling.

Roll out one dough and put into a 9" pie dish. Don't prebake. In a large bowl combine the apples and lemon juice. Mix the remaining ingredients, except the butter and egg wash. Add to apples. Put apple filling into the unbaked pie crust. Dot fruit with 2 T of butter. Roll out the remaining dough and cover the top of the pie. Leave about 2" of overhang and cut off the rest. Brush bottom dough edge with egg wash and pinch together the bottom and the top edge. Fold up and roll in, pinching the edges with your fingers. If you have any extra dough left over, cut out an apple shape with a branch and leaves and add to top for decoration. Coat pie with egg wash. Slice 4 slits into the top crust and bake.

Bake for 15 minutes at 425°.
Reduce heat to 350° and bake 30 – 45 minutes, or until crust is golden brown and filling bubbles. Be sure to put a piece of foil under pie to catch spills as it bakes.

Paonia Peach Crisp
Gluten free

GF, DF & VG

Serves 8 -10
10 C peaches - peeled and sliced
1 T arrowroot
2 lemons - juiced
½ C sugar
½ tsp cinnamon or ground gringer

Fill a 2 gallon stock pot with water and bring to a boil. Cut an **X** on the top of each peach. Drop peaches into boiling water and remove when skin starts to peel (about 1 minute). Peel, pit and slice peaches. (Or you can peel the peaches with a paring knife and slice.) Put lemon juice in a large bowl, add sliced peaches (this will keep the peaches from browning). Take 2 T of juice from the bowl and add the arrowroot. Mix well and add back to the peaches. Add the remaining ingredients.

Oil or spray Pam® on a 9 x 13 glass or ceramic baking dish. Add the peach mix. Top with crumble mix (below)

Crumble Mix
¾ C sugar
¼ C brown sugar
½ C rice flour
¼ C tapioca flour
½ C gluten free oats
¼ tsp kosher salt
½ C Earth Balance® (or butter if you prefer dairy)
1 tsp cinnamon

Topping
¾ C oats - gluten free
¾ C sliced almonds

Preheat oven to 350°.
Pulse all of the crumble mix ingredients in a food processor until Earth Balance® or butter is mixed well. Add to the top of the peaches in the baking dish. Top with the remaining ½ C oats and ¼ C sliced almonds.

Bake uncovered for approximately 1 hour until topping is golden brown and peach filling is bubbling.

Paonia Peaches - Peaches from Paonia, Colorado are western slope favorites. You can use any farmers market peach for this recipe. I prefer to use the freestone peaches, because they are easy to peel and pit. They come out later in the season.

Nut Allergies: Omit the almonds.

Arrowroot - Is a powdered tropical root starch that is used as a thickener. It is prefered over cornstarch. It is non GMO and not highly processed. A great substitute for those allergic to wheat and corn.

Collections from an Aspen Chef ~ Cindy Rogers

Lee's Raspberry Galette
With Whipped Cream

Lee is a client and friend, I've named this dessert Lee's because it's one of her favorites. She and I have worked on this recipe for years to get it just right.

Serves 8 -10

Sweet Pie Crust
2½ C flour
¼ C sugar
¼ tsp kosher salt
2 sticks cold unsalted butter, cut into small pieces
2 large egg yolks (save the whites to brush on crust)
4 T cold water (up to ½ C)

Line a sheet pan with parchment. Make crust at least 1 hour ahead.

Preheat oven to 350°.
In mixer, add dry ingredients. While motor is running on low, add the butter and mix until you have small crumbles. Add egg yolks and mix. With mixer running, add 4 T cold water. If the dough isn't coming together, slowly add more cold water, 1 T at a time until the dough is incorporated and forms a ball. Be sure not to add too much water. You want the dough firm, not slippery.

Form dough into a rectangular shape ¾" tall. Refrigerate for 1 hour or up to 2 days, or freeze up to 1 month.

Filling
6 (4.4 oz) containers fresh raspberries
¼ C sugar
zest of 1 lemon
1 tsp cinnamon (optional)
2 T butter - to dot the fruit
1 egg yolk and 2 T heavy cream - for the egg wash

Mix the raspberry filling in a bowl. Set aside.

Roll out dough on a sheet of parchment with a little bit of flour. Roll large enough to overhang a sheet pan. Leave it on the parchment paper and place on sheet pan. Brush the rolled out dough with the egg whites and allow to dry. Add the filling and fold the crust edges on top of the fruit. Pinch the corners to hold crust. (Most of the fruit is still exposed, with the freeform crust around the edges.) Dot the fruit with the remaining 2 T butter.

Brush the top and edges with the egg wash and sprinkle with a little sugar.
Bake at 350° for 45 minutes or until the top is golden brown.

Blueberry Cobbler
Gluten Free

GF

I have a client who tries to eat clean, but loves really good desserts. He asked me to not tell him how healthy this dessert is. (I make it GF & DF.) He preferred to enjoy it, as if full of all the things he tries to stay away from.

Serves 8 -10

Filling
8 (6oz) containers blueberries and blackberries - 6 blue, 2 black
½ C brown sugar
3 T rice flour
1 T grated orange zest
1 T grated lemon zest
4 tsp orange juice concentrate

Preheat oven to 350°. Spray 9 x 11 baking dish with Pam®. Mix filling by hand. Add to baking dish.

Gluten Free Biscuits
¾ C rice flour
½ C potato starch
¼ C cornstarch
2 tsp xanthan gum
½ C sugar
2½ tsp baking powder
½ tsp baking soda
¼ tsp kosher salt
1 egg
½ C buttermilk
6 T butter
½ tsp vanilla

Topping
¼ C slivered almonds- optional
¼ C oats - GF

Dairy Free Option :
I prefer coconut milk in the carton in place of buttermilk. Use coconut oil or Earth Balance® in place of butter.

Nut allergies:
Omit the almonds.

Gluten Free Oats -
Check the label, some oats are processed in a facility with wheat. If someone has Celiac disease, you need to be really careful.

Corn Free Option:
Use tapioca flour in place of corn starch.

Mix the dry ingredients in a mixer, then add wet ingredients. Mix just until your biscuit mix is incorporated (this will be gooey) – don't over mix. Add dollops of biscuit mix (about ¼ cup each) to the top of the berry mix. Be sure to leave about half inch or more of space between dollops. Top with slivered almonds and oats.

Bake at 350° for 25-30 minutes, until biscuits are golden brown and fruit is bubbling.

Vegan Chocolate Mousse
With Avocados

GF, DF & VG

I came up with this dessert for my friend Nancy on her birthday one year. She has Celiac disease and loves chocolate desserts. I wanted to make something she could enjoy.

Serves 8

1 ripe avocado
¼ C cocoa powder
¼ C maple syrup
1 T coconut oil - soft or melted
1 T vanilla
1 (13.66 oz) can coconut milk - refrigerated for at least 2 hours to harden and separate milk solids from liquid

4 oz dairy free dark chocolate bar (Green & Black's® makes one)
¼ C coconut milk (from remaining liquid in the can)

Put avocado, cocoa powder, maple syrup, coconut oil, and vanilla into a food processor and pulse until blended and smooth. Place in a bowl.

Take the can of coconut milk out of the refrigerator and scoop out the solidified portion from the can into a bowl. Reserve ¼ C of the remaining liquid. Whip with an electric mixer until doubled in size.

In a double boiler (see sidebar pg. 146) or microwave, melt the dairy free dark chocolate bar. When completely melted remove from heat and add remaining coconut liquid. Whisk until combined.

Fold the whipped coconut solids into the ingredients that have been pureed in the food processor. Then gently fold chocolate and reserved coconut liquid to the mix.

Hold in the refrigerator until ready to enjoy!

Coconut Milk - When using coconut milk in the can, I prefer to use Thai Kitchen® Coconut Milk, Unsweetened. Its fat content solidifies well.

Coconut Milk in a Can vs. Carton - There is a big difference between coconut milk in a can vs. in a carton. At the time of this publication, So Delicious® Coconut Milk, (in a carton) is the only unflavored coconut milk that is the closest replacement to cow's milk. It also is my favorite dairy free substitute. Canned coconut milk has a distinctive coconut flavor with high sugar and fat contents. Great for desserts.

Coconut Mini Loaf Cakes
With Vegan Cream Cheese Frosting

 DF

I try to always have these in my freezer, my friends love them and it's a nice way to say thank you for all the wonderful things they do for me!

Makes 4 mini loaves

½ C turbinado sugar - to coat the pans
½ C coconut oil - softened, plus ¼ C to coat the pans
¾ C sugar
2 eggs
1 C Baker's® Angel Flake coconut, sweetened
½ C unsweetened large flake coconut
½ C cream of coconut (15 oz can Coco Lopez® - use half of can, freeze the other half)
¼ C Malibu® coconut rum
½ C So Delicious® Coconut Milk
1 tsp baking powder
½ tsp kosher salt
1½ C flour

Preheat oven to 325°.
Coat 4 mini loaf pans with soft coconut oil, using a paper towel to spread. Then pour on turbinado sugar to coat pans. Discard the loose turbinado sugar.

Mix ½ C coconut oil and sugar in a mixer. Add eggs. Then add the rest of the ingredients. Pour into 4 mini loaf pans and bake for a total of 50 minutes. Rotate after 25 minutes. Or use one full size loaf pan and bake 1 hour. Rotate after 30 minutes.

Vegan Cream Cheese Frosting

❄ GF, DF & VG

1 stick Earth Balance®
1 (8 oz) container Tofutti® Better Than Cream Cheese - softened
1 lb powdered sugar
1 tsp vanilla

Whip the Earth Balance®, Tofutti® Better Than Cream Cheese and vanilla in a mixer. Add powdered sugar and mix until soft. Spread on top of loaves, only! You want to enjoy the turbinado sugar crust on the sides.

Will keep in freezer for a few months.

Chocolate Layered Mousse Cake
With GF & DF Options

Serves 25

Cake

3 C flour
⅔ C unsweetened cocoa powder
2 tsp baking soda
2 C sugar
1 tsp kosher salt
2 C cold water
1 C + 2 T canola oil
1 T vanilla
2 T cider vinegar

Mix both wet dry ingredients in a bowl. Beat on medium speed for 1 minute.
Grease and flour one 13 x 9 pan, or three 8" round pans. Bake at 350° for 25-30 minutes.

Chocolate Mousse Filling
8 oz semi sweet chocolate
1 egg
2 egg yolks
2 egg whites - beaten stiff
1 C heavy cream - whipped
3 T powdered sugar

Melt the chocolate in a double boiler. Remove from heat. Add 1 egg and mix. Beat in 2 egg yolks and whisk for 4-5 minutes. Fold in beaten egg whites and heavy cream whipped with powdered sugar.
Can make ahead. This will hold for 10 days in the refrigerator.

> **Vegan Filling Option:**
> Use the vegan chocolate mousse on pg 134.
>
> **Vegan Frosting Option:**
> Use the Chocolate Ganache Recipe on pg 139, using coconut milk in place of whipping cream.

Chocolate Frosting

8 oz unsweetened chocolate - Scharffen Berger® chocolate is my favorite
½ C (1 stick) butter
2 C powered sugar
½ C heavy cream or coconut milk
⅛ tsp kosher salt
1 tsp vanilla

Melt chocolate in a double boiler (see sidebar pg. 137). Cool. In a stand mixer, beat butter, powdered sugar, salt and vanilla. Slowly add melted chocolate then cream. Mix until soft peaks form. If frosting is too soft let stand at room temperature, about 1 hour. Whip to the desired consistency.

Chocolate Eruptions
With Vanilla Ice Cream

 GF

One of my favorite clients in Aspen and LA covets these delicious chocolate treats.

Serves 12
6 T unsalted butter- softened, plus more to coat ramekins
12 oz semisweet chocolate
5 large eggs - separated
10 T sugar
½ tsp vanilla extract
Chocolate truffles (recipe below)

> **Double Boiler -**
> You can make your own by using a sauce pan half filled with simmering water and a metal or glass bowl that sits tightly on top to capture the steam from the hot water. This method is used to heat delicate ingredients you don't want to bind or burn.

Make the Chocolate truffles ahead of time and keep in the freezer.

Butter 12 small ramekins (about 3" across). Set aside.

Melt butter and chocolate in a double boiler. Set aside.
Combine egg yolks and 6 T sugar in a mixer bowl. Beat until pale yellow and thick, about 5 minutes. Stir in vanilla, then add melted chocolate mixture to egg yolk mixture and beat on low, about 30 seconds. Don't overmix!

Whip egg whites until frothy. Add remaining 4 T sugar, whip until soft peaks form. Fold into chocolate mixture.

Fill bottom of ramekins with chocolate mixture, about 2 T. Add a chocolate truffle ball to the center. Cover with chocolate mixture, just below the top rim of the ramekins.

Freeze, then cover with plastic wrap until ready to bake. These will hold in the freezer for up to a month.

Preheat oven to 350°. Take eruptions out of the freezer and place directly onto a sheet pan and into the oven. Bake 20-25 minutes until tops pop up and look firm. Don't let them burn. Serve with vanilla ice cream.

Chocolate Truffles
4 oz semi sweet chocolate
¾ C heavy cream

Melt the chocolate in a double boiler (see sidebar above). Remove from heat and add the heavy cream. Whisk thoroughly to combine. Place in freezer for about 45 minutes until mixture starts to firm up. With the large side of a melon baller, scoop 1" balls and cover with plastic wrap. Freeze until ready to use.

Meringue Holiday Mushrooms
For the Bûche de Noël or Holiday Yule Log

GF & DF

Thanks to my friend Iris for leading me down this path. It was easier than I thought!

Makes about 15 mushrooms
3 large egg whites - room temperature
¾ C sugar
unsweetened cocoa powder and paprika for dusting mushrooms
1 egg white - room temperature, plus 2 T sugar - to use later for assembly glue

Preheat oven to 200°. Most recipes will call for 180°, it's hard to set most ovens that low.

Whip egg whites in a mixer until stiff, add sugar. Beat until meringue holds stiff glossy peaks.

Put into a pastry bag with a ½ inch plain tip. Pipe half the meringue mix into 2½ inch round mounds, to make it look like a mushroom cap. You will shave the points off later so don't worry about being perfect. Pipe the other half into conical stems about 1" tall. To make the stems, start out fat on the bottom with a tapered finish (the tip will later be used to go into the cap).
Bake for 2 hours, or until firm to the touch. Check at 1 hour to make sure they are not cooking too fast. Turn the oven off and let them remain inside the oven overnight.

Preheat oven to 200°.
Egg Glue - Beat the remaining egg white stiff. Add 2 T sugar and continue beating until glossy peaks form.

Assemble - Take a sharp paring knife and shave the top of the mushroom cap smooth. Then dip your finger in a little bit of water to smooth the cap and give it a nice smooth mushroom finish. Use a sharp paring knife to carve a hole in the center of the base of each groomed cap. Take the tip of the stem and apply some of the egg glue (above). Also put some of the egg glue into the hole you have carved in the cap. Gently hold the cap on the stem and allow the glue to set. Carefully place onto a parchment lined cookie sheet. Continue with the rest of the mushroom assembly. When done put the cookie sheet into your preheated oven and turn off. Let set in the oven for an hour.

Dust with paprika and cocoa powder to decorate.

The mushrooms will keep at room temperature in an airtight container for 1 - 3 days. Do not refrigerate. In climates with high humidity, serve immediately - these won't hold their crispy state.

Bûchë de Noël - Yule Log Cake
With Chocolate Mousse Filling

GF

I make this every year for various client's Christmas parties. It makes quite a presentation on a platter with the Lindzor cookies, pg. 154.

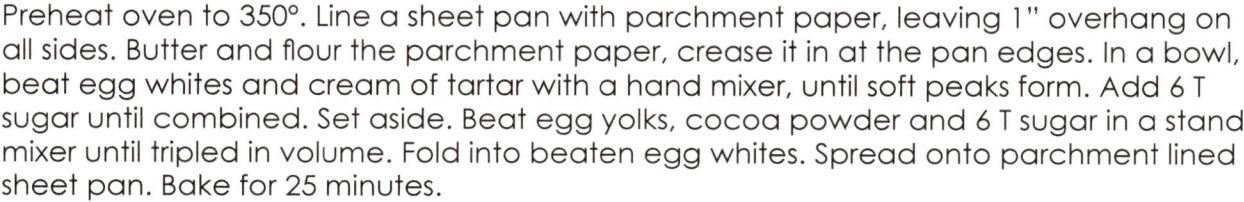

❄ GF & DF

Serves 18
Cake
6 eggs separated
½ tsp cream of tartar
12 T sugar
⅓ C unsweetened cocoa powder
plus extra cocoa powder and powdered sugar to dust cheesecloth and roulade

Preheat oven to 350°. Line a sheet pan with parchment paper, leaving 1" overhang on all sides. Butter and flour the parchment paper, crease it in at the pan edges. In a bowl, beat egg whites and cream of tartar with a hand mixer, until soft peaks form. Add 6 T sugar until combined. Set aside. Beat egg yolks, cocoa powder and 6 T sugar in a stand mixer until tripled in volume. Fold into beaten egg whites. Spread onto parchment lined sheet pan. Bake for 25 minutes.

Filling– Chocolate mousse pg. 136.

Assemble
Lay a cheesecloth dish towel on a flat counter. Dust with powdered sugar and cocoa powder. Invert the cake onto the powdered cheesecloth - carefully remove the parchment paper and remove the hard crusty edges of cake with a knife. Then dust with powdered sugar and cocoa powder and roll up. Leave rolled until cool. Then unroll and apply mousse in a thin layer on the cake. Gently use your cheesecloth to facilitate the roll, rolling the cake from the long side onto the mousse layer to form a roulade. Wrap in plastic wrap and freeze until ready to frost with the ganache.

Ganache
❄ GF

6 oz bittersweet chocolate
2 T corn syrup
1 T Grand Marnier® or brandy
½ C whipping cream
If you prefer it to be more bitter add 2 – 3 T unsweetened cocoa powder.

Melt chocolate, Grand Marnier and corn syrup in a double boiler (see sidebar pg. 137). Remove from heat. Add cream and let stand until cool. Whip until soft peaks form. Frost yule log cake, then use a fork to make marks like bark. You can cut an end off of the cake at an angle and add it to the main log to look like a tree branch. Blend the seam with ganache. Garnish with Meringue mushrooms, pg.138.

Collections from an Aspen Chef ~ Cindy Rogers

Vegan Cheesecake
With a Raspberry Coulis and Vegan Cool Whip

DF & VG

This Recipe was shared with me by my sister-in-law and her sisters. I've made some changes, to accommodate my love for lemons and a raspberry coulis with different crust options.

Serves 8

Crust
3 C graham crackers
4 T sugar
½ C Earth Balance® or coconut oil - melted

Chop graham crackers and sugar in a food processor until fine. Add melted Earth Balance® or coconut oil. Press crust mixture into 9 or 9½" pie dish. Use a measuring cup to press the mixture firmly down in pie dish. Bake at 350° for 10-12 minutes.

Filling
2 (8 oz) containers Tofutti® Better Than Cream Cheese
½ C sugar
¼ C + 2 T lemon juice
½ tsp vanilla extract
pinch of kosher salt
1 T potato starch
1 T tapioca flour

Gluten Free Option: You can use gluten free graham crackers.

Or

Gluten Free Crust:
3 C ground almonds
¼ C sugar
¼ C + 2 T coconut oil - melted. Follow same instructions.

Nut Allergies: Don't use second option!

Preheat oven to 350°. Beat Tofutti ®Bettter Than Cream Cheese at medium speed in a mixer until smooth. Add sugar, salt, lemon juice, and vanilla extract, beat 1 minute. Add tapioca flour and potato starch. Continue beating until smooth and pour into crust. Bake at 350° for 30–35 minutes until set. Cool to room temperature. Refrigerate. The pie needs to be completely chilled before serving.

Vegan Whipped Frosting

❄ **GF, DF & VG**

1 (13.66 oz) can coconut milk, unsweetened - fat part only
¼ C powdered sugar
¼ tsp vanilla extract

Put can of coconut milk in the refrigerator for 3 hours to solidify and separate. Remove the solidified fat portion from the can and discard the rest.
Whip the fat part of the coconut milk in a mixer until doubled in size. Add powdered sugar and vanilla. Spread on top of cheesecake and top with fresh berries and serve each piece on a puddle of raspberry coulis pg 147.

Grandma's Classic Cheesecake
With a Graham Cracker Crust

Serves 15

You need a 12" springform pan.
Preheat oven to 325°.

Crust
3 C graham crackers
4 T sugar
½ C melted butter

Chop graham crackers and sugar in a food processor until fine. Add melted butter. Press crust mixture into a 12" spring form pan. Chill 30 minutes.

Filling
5 (8 oz) pkgs Philadelphia® Original Cream Cheese – softened
1⅓ C sugar
3 T flour
3 lg eggs
½ C sour cream
2 tsp lemon peel - finely grated
1½ tsp vanilla

Beat cream cheese at medium speed in a mixer until smooth, add sugar. Gradually add flour. Mix until combined. On low speed add eggs, one at a time. Beat another minute. Add sour cream, lemon peel and vanilla. Beat until blended.

Pour into crust. Bake 1 hr 15 minutes.
Remove the cheesecake from oven.
Reset oven to 425°.

Topping
1½ C sour cream
2 T sugar
½ tsp vanilla
⅛ tsp kosher salt

Mix ingredients and add to the top of the cheesecake; be sure to spread it over the crust edge, or it will pull away during baking. Bake 5 minutes. Take out of oven and cool to room temperature.
Refrigerate 6–12 hours before serving. Will hold in the refrigerator for 5 days.

> **Gluten Free Option:** For the crust, you can use gluten free graham crackers.
>
> Replace flour in the filling with 1½ T potato starch and 1½ T tapioca starch.

Bananas Foster
A la Mode

GF

This dessert is delicious, but warn your guest, IT HAS ALCOHOL!

Serves 6

¼ C (½ stick) unsalted butter
¼ C dark brown sugar
4 bananas - peeled and sliced on diagonal
¼ tsp cinnamon
3 T banana cordial
¼ C Meyers® rum
vanilla ice cream

> **Dairy Free Option:** Use coconut oil to sauté and Coconut Bliss® ice cream in place of vanilla ice cream.

Melt the butter in a 12" skillet. Add the sugar and mix until incorporated. Add the bananas and cinnamon. Sauté until the bananas are crispy and golden brown. Deglaze the pan with rum and banana cordial. Reduce until the mix is syrupy.

Remove from heat and serve over vanilla ice cream.

Key Lime Pie
With Chocolate Wafer Crust

Serves 10 - 12

Crust
1½ -2 C Nabisco's® Famous Chocolate Wafers, 9 oz box (¾ of a box)
2 T sugar
¼ C (½ stick) melted butter

> **Gluten Free Option:** Use GF graham crackers in place of wafers.

Chop chocolate wafers and sugar in a food processor until fine. Add melted butter. Press into 9 or 9½" pie dish. Use a measuring cup to press the mixture firmly down in pie dish.

Key Lime Filling   GF
2 (14 oz) cans condensed milk
6 egg yolks (save the whites for the meringue)
1 C Nellie & Joe's® Key West Lime Juice (in a plastic lime green bottle at grocery stores)

Preheat oven to 350°. Blend all the ingredients in a mixer and pour into the pie crust. Bake at 350° for 20 minutes. Take out and cool before topping with meringue. I like to do this a day ahead, cover with plastic and put in the refrigerator.

French Meringue Topping   GF & DF
6 egg whites
¾ tsp cream of tartar
9 T Sugar
1 tsp vanilla

Whip egg whites in a mixer until frothy. Add cream of tartar. Whip until stiff but not dry. Beat in sugar, 1 T at a time. Beat in vanilla. Using a creme brulee torch, brown the peaks.

Italian Meringue Topping   GF & DF
1¼ C sugar
¼ C water
6 egg whites
¼ tsp cream of tartar
2 tsp corn starch
2 T powdered sugar

Heat the sugar and water in a heavy-bottomed pan until it reaches 240° on a candy thermometer. Don't stir. Swirl the pan to wash down the crystals.

Beat egg whites in a mixer until frothy. Add cream of tartar, corn starch and powdered sugar. Beat until stiff, but not dry.

With the mixer on medium, quickly add the 240° sugar water to the stiff egg whites. Whip on high until glossy, about 5 minutes. Apply to top of cooled key lime pie, taking meringue over the edges. This will keep the pie from oozing out. Using a creme brulee torch, brown the peaks.

Mini Key Lime Frozen Treats
With Candied Lemon Zest

GF & DF

My friend Jules and I came up with this delicious treat on the Big Island of Hawaii after our friend Colleen brought us a jar of her "Just MacNuts, Raw Butta'® (macadamia nut butter) and another friend Marian brought us fresh key limes from her orchard.

Makes enough for 18 medium muffin liners
You will need 2 muffin trays: one for 12 and one for 6. A day ahead: place can of coconut milk in the refrigerator to harden the milk solids.

Crust:

GF & DF

2 C graham crackers – GF & DF
¼ C coconut oil – melted
1 T sugar
1 package of foil/paper muffin liners.

> **GF & DF Cookies (in place of graham crackers) -**
> I prefer Pamela's®, Small Bites-Ginger Snapz, mini cookies - 7oz bag. Use 1½ bags and omit the sugar.

Preheat oven to 350°. Line 18 muffin tins with foil liners.
Chop graham crackers in a food processor until a fine crumb. Add melted coconut oil and sugar. Place 1½ T of crust mixture into each liner. Then firmly press down using a glass that fits into muffin liner. Bake for 6 minutes. Cool.

Filling:

❄ **GF, DF & VG**

¾ C key lime juice – fresh or Nellie & Joe's® Famous Key West Lime Juice
1 C Just MacNuts - Raw Butta'® (pg 10) or 1 C raw cashew butter
¼ C coconut oil
1 (13.66 oz) can full fat coconut milk, unsweetened
½ C honey

Place all the ingredients in a Cuisinart® or Vita-mixer®. Purée until a fine blend.
Pour into muffin liners with the cooled graham cracker crust.
Place in the freezer for 2-4 hours.

Topping:

❄ **GF, DF & VG**

1 (13.66 oz) can full fat coconut milk, unsweetened
¼ C powdered sugar

Take the can of coconut milk out of the refrigerator and scoop out the solidified portion from the can into a bowl. Discard the remaining liquid.

With an electric mixer, whip coconut solids and powdered sugar until it thickens to a whipped cream texture. Spoon equally on top of the frozen key lime treats. (About 1 T per treat). Put back in the freezer. Freeze another 2 hours. Take out 15 minutes before serving to soften. Will keep covered for 2 weeks in freezer.

Garnish - with candied lemon zest (pg 145).

Candied Lemon Zest
For Garnish

GF, DF & VG

4 lemons well scrubbed
2 C sugar
1 C cool water

Remove rind from lemons with a potato peeler, keeping pieces long. Remove white pith using a paring knife. Cut zest into a fine julienne using a very sharp knife. Place julienne lemon stips in a small bowl, cover with boiling water. Let stand 30 minutes and drain.

In a small saucepan bring sugar and cool water to a boil over medium heat. When sugar is dissolved, add zest. Reduce heat to medium low and cook 25 minutes. Remove from heat, take lemon strips out of syrup and toss into a bowl of sugar. Remove lemon strips from sugar and cool on a sheet of parchment paper. Store in an airtight container in the refrigerator for up to 2 weeks.

This is great for anything that calls for a sweet lemon garnish!

Lemon Cake with Seven Minute Icing
With a Lemon Curd Filling

Serves 20

Preheat oven to 350°. Grease and flour two 9" round pans. Line with parchment paper.

Lemon Curd Filling　　　　　　　　　　　　　　　　　　　　　　　　　　　GF
4 eggs
1 C sugar
2 lemons juiced
½ C (1 stick) unsalted butter
zest of 2 lemons

Put all ingredients into a sauce pan and heat on medium. Whisk until thick, 5 -10 minutes. Cover with plastic directly on surface. Refrigerate for at least 4 hours or up to 3 days ahead.

Lemon Chiffon Cake　　　　　　　　　　　　　　　　　　　　　　　　　　　DF
6 eggs - separated
1½ C flour
½ tsp baking soda
½ tsp salt
1½ C + 1T sugar
½ C canola oil
⅔ C water
4 T lemon zest
2 T lemon juice
1 tsp vanilla
½ tsp cream of tartar

Double Boiler - You can make your own by using a sauce pan half filled with simmering water and a metal or glass bowl that sits tightly on top to capture the steam from the hot water. This method is used to heat delicate ingredients you don't want to bind or burn.

Whip egg whites until stiff but not dry. Add 1 T sugar, set aside. In a separate bowl add the rest of the ingredients and mix on high for 5 minutes. Fold into the stiff egg whites. Place in two 9" round pans. Bake for 25–30 minutes at 350° until done. Cool for 1½ hrs. Cut each cake in half horizontally through the middle with a serrated knife. This will give you four round cake pieces. Fill the first 3 layers with lemon curd. Place on cake stand with strips of parchment underneath to catch the mess while icing cake with Seven Minute Icing (below).

Seven Minute Icing　　　　　　　　　　　　　　　　　　　　　　　　　　GF & DF
2 large egg whites
1C sugar
¼ C water
1 T juice from lemon
1 T corn syrup

Combine all ingredients in a metal bowl on top of a double-boiler on medium heat, stirring constantly until candy thermometer reads 160°. Add to mixing bowl and whip on medium until soft peaks form, 5–10 minutes. Mix on high another 5 minutes until it reaches room temperature. Frost the lemon curd layered cake. This cake can be refrigerated 1 day ahead before serving.

Lemon Lime Tart
With Kiwi & Berry Topping

Serves 12

You need a 10" Tart pan. Preheat oven to 350°

Crust
1½ C flour
½ C almond flour
½ C (1 stick butter) unsalted butter
5 T sugar
1 large egg yolk
1 tsp lemon zest
½ tsp vanilla
⅓ C water

> **Gluten Free Crust option:**
> 3 C ground almonds
> ¼ C sugar
> ¼ C + 2 T coconut oil - melted.
> Follow same instructions.
>
> If there are nut allergies, this isn't an option!

Mix all the ingredients of the crust in a mixer, except the water. When crumbly, slowly add the water to combine the dough. Roll out dough and place in a tart pan. Freeze 10 minutes. Bake at 350° with pie weights for 15 minutes, until crust is set. Remove pie weights and bake until golden brown, about 25 minutes. Take out of oven and cool. Can be prepared 1 day ahead. Cover and store at room temperature.

Filling   GF
5 large eggs
1 large egg yolk
1 C sugar
⅔ C whipping cream
2½ T fresh lemon juice
2 T fresh lime juice
1½ T lemon zest
1 T lime zest

> **Pie Weights -**
> Are used to hold pastry dough down while you bake pie crust, before adding filling. You can use bulk beans or buy weights at a kitchen store or online.

Topping - 1 pint each - raspberries, blackberries, strawberries, blueberries and kiwi fruit.

Whisk eggs, yolk and sugar in a mixer. Gradually add cream, lemon and lime juices and zests. Pour filling into prepared crust. Bake at 350° until filling is set, about 40 minutes. Cool to room temperature. Sprinkle with powdered sugar. Top with sliced kiwi fruit, raspberries, blackberries and strawberries. Cover the entire top with fruit.

Raspberry Coulis Sauce   GF, DF & VG
1 bag frozen raspberries
¼ C powdered sugar

Puree raspberries in a food processor, strain through a chinois strainer (a conical sieve with very fine mesh) to remove seeds. Add powdered sugar. Refrigerate until needed.

Pour a puddle of coulis sauce onto a plate. Add slice of tart and more berries. Serve.

Lemon Pudding Cakes
From the Freezer to the Oven

GF & DF

These are great if you want to have something quick and easy to pull out of the freezer and bake for dessert.

Serves 8
3 lg egg whites
2 lg egg yolks
¾ C + ¼ C sugar
¼ C rice flour
1 T tapioca flour
½ tsp xanthan gum
⅛ tsp kosher salt
1 C coconut milk - in the carton pg. 8
2 T coconut oil - melted
½ C lemon juice
2 tsp lemon zest

Gluten Option: If you can tolerate gluten use ⅓ C flour in place of the rice flour, tapioca flour and xanthan gum.

Grease 8 small ramekins (about 3¼" across).

Beat the egg yolks and ¾ C sugar in a mixer for 5 minutes until pale yellow. Add flours, xanthan gum, salt, coconut milk, coconut oil, lemon juice and zest.

In a separate bowl, whip the egg whites until stiff. Add ¼ C sugar. Fold the stiff egg whites into the other mixed ingredients. Pour into greased ramekins and place into the freezer unbaked. Cover with plastic wrap after frozen.

Preheat oven to 350°.
From the freezer, place frozen ramekins onto a sheet pan and into the oven. Bake 20 minutes. Serve.

Or if you want to eat them right away, place ramekins on sheet pan. Bake 20 minutes.

Poached pears
In a Pomegranate/Açai Port Sauce

GF, DF & VG

Serves 6

8 whole allspice
1 T pink peppercorns
1" to 2" piece fresh ginger, peeled and sliced into ⅛" pieces
1" to 2" cinnamon stick
1 whole orange - peeled with a potato peeler
3 C pomegranate/açai juice
2 C tawny port
½ C cherries dried
½ C sugar

6 ripe Anjou pears with stems

Tie allspice and peppercorns in a cheesecloth. Bring all ingredients, except pears, to a boil. Simmer for 15 minutes.

Peel pears and add to the sauce, gently keep rotating sides, turning every 10 minutes, for about 40 minutes.

Remove pears, take spice cheesecloth out and reduce sauce for 15 minutes.

Serve pears with ice cream and sauce on top.

Chocolate Peanut Butter Torte
With a Chocolate Wafer Crust

Serves 12 - Make torte day ahead to set. Allow 6 hours for finished torte to set before serving.

Crust
3 C Nabisco's® Famous Chocolate Wafers (get 2 boxes, you will need about 1½ boxes)
4 T sugar
½ C butter - melted

> **Gluten Free Option:** Use GF graham crackers in place of wafers.

Grease 11" tart pan with removable bottom. Chop chocolate wafers and sugar in a food processor until fine. Add melted butter. Transfer to tart pan, be sure to press a good side wall then press the bottom firmly down.

Filling   GF
¼ C unsalted butter
½ C brown sugar
pinch of kosher salt
½ C heavy whipping cream
⅓ C honey
1 C lightly salted dry roasted peanuts

Melt butter in heavy saucepan over medium heat. Whisk in brown sugar and salt, then cream and honey. Bring to rolling boil and cook 1 minute, swirling pan occasionally. Stir in 1 C peanuts. Pour filling into crust. Bake at 350° for exactly 15 minutes. Remove and cool for 2 hours. Then freeze for 15 minutes. Place in the refrigerator until ready to use.

Candied Peanuts - for topping   GF & DF
1 egg white
6 T sugar
1½ C raw Virginia peanuts

Preheat oven to 350°. Mix all ingredients. Place on foil-lined baking sheet. Bake about 10 minutes, until peanuts are light brown and caramelized. Set aside.

Peanut Butter Frosting   GF
2 C powdered sugar
⅔ C unsalted peanut butter (Arrowhead Mills ®)
4 – 5 T milk or more to acheive a thin spreadable consistency

Beat all the ingredients in a mixer until smooth. When torte is cool, add a layer of peanut butter frosting. Leave enough room for the chocolate ganache. You may not need all the frosting.

Chocolate Ganache   GF
9.7 oz Scharffen Berger® bittersweet dark chocolate bar
¾ C heavy whipping cream

Melt the chocolate in a double boiler. Take off heat, whisk in the whipping cream. Cool slightly. Pour on top of the torte. Add the candied peanuts to the top and refrigerate for 6 hours to set.

Collections from an Aspen Chef ~ Cindy Rogers

Raspberry Lemon Trifle
With a Lemon Curd Filling

GF

If you have a really cool glass trifle bowl, this dessert looks amazing! I use a 10" cylindrical glass bowl that includes a stand.

Serves 12

1 (16oz) frozen Sara Lee® pound cake - thaw

> **Gluten Free Option:**
> Use a frozen GF pound cake. Or bake from a mix (Bob's Red Mill® GF pound cake mix).

Syrup

GF, DF & VG

½ C sugar
⅓ C fresh lemon juice
¼ C water

Combine sugar, lemon juice, and water in saucepan. Bring to a boil and stir until sugar dissolves. Reduce heat to medium-low and simmer 1 minute. Cover and chill.

Lemon Curd

GF

4 lg eggs
1 C sugar
⅓ C fresh lemon juice
½ C (1 stick) unsalted butter
1 T grated lemon peel

Whisk eggs, sugar and lemon juice in heavy saucepan to blend. Add butter and lemon peel. Stir over medium heat until curd thickens, about 7 minutes. Transfer to small bowl, cover surface with plastic wrap. Chill at least 4 hours. Can be made 3 days ahead.

Fruit & Topping

GF

8 (½-pint) baskets fresh raspberries
¼ C + 3 T sugar
2 C chilled whipping cream

Coarsely mash 4 baskets of raspberries and ¼ C sugar with a fork. Let stand for 30 minutes. Stir occasionally.

Slice cake into 8 pieces. Cut each piece into 3 strips. Line bottom of a 3 quart trifle bowl with 8 cake strips. Drizzle with 3 T syrup, spread ⅔ C curd, then half the mashed berries and 1½ baskets of whole raspberries. Repeat layering. Top with remaining cake, syrup and curd. Cover and chill overnight.

Whip the cream until soft peaks form, add 3 T sugar. Mound some over trifle and top with some of the remaining fresh berries. Use the remaining whipped cream and berries to top each serving.

Collections from an Aspen Chef
Favorite recipes with options to accommodate your dietary preferences

GF = Gluten Free ~ DF = Dairy Free ~ VG = Vegan ~ ❄ = Freezes Well

Collections from an Aspen Chef
Favorite recipes with options to accommodate your dietary preferences

Cookies & Holiday Egg Nog:

Dutch Star Spice Cookies with Lemon Icing	154
Crunchy Chocolate/Butterscotch Chip Cookies	155
Oatmeal Cherry Cookies	156
Ginger Bread People	157
Linzer Cookies	158
Sugar Cookies w/Royal Icing	159
Bernice's Pecan Slices	160
Aunt Libby's Bourbon Balls	161
Pecan Balls Rolled in Powdered Sugar	162
Chocolate Gluten Free Cookies w/Caramel	163
Chocolate Peanut Butter Brownies	164
Lemon Bars	165
Biscotti	166
1960's Holiday Egg Nog	167

Dutch Star Spice Cookies
With Cindy's Lemon Royal Icing

Makes approximately 48 small star cookies

1 C (2 sticks) unsalted butter - softened
1 C brown sugar
½ C almonds – grind in a food processor
2⅔ C flour
2 tsp cinnamon - ground
1 tsp cloves - ground
½ tsp baking powder
½ tsp nutmeg - whole, finely grated
½ tsp kosher salt
3 ½ T Meyers® Rum

Preheat oven to 350°. Parchment line a sheet pan.
Beat the butter and sugar until creamy. Add the rest of the ingredients. Roll out between two parchment sheets. Cut with small star cookie cutter. Bake for 10 minutes. Remove and place on cooling racks. Decorate with royal icing.

Cindy's Lemon Royal Icing
Since the scare with Salmonella, I started using dehydrated egg whites that are also listed as meringue powder. It has been pasteurized. You can find this online at King Arthur Flour® or in some specialty grocery stores.

¼ C dehydrated egg whites
¾ C + 2 T water
2 lemons - juiced
2 lbs powdered sugar

Whisk the egg whites, water and lemon juice in a mixer until stiff peaks form. Add powdered sugar and whisk until smooth.

Dairy Free Option:
Use Earth Balance® in place of the butter.

Parchment Paper -
I like to roll out my cookie dough between 2 full size sheets of parchment paper without flour. If you use flour, it adds to the dough, making the second roll out strange. Then the cookies aren't as pretty and taste heavier.

Whole Nutmeg -
To finely grate whole nutmeg use a nutmeg grater. They are easy to find online. Freshly grated nutmeg goes a long way and is worth the effort.

Chocolate Chip Butterscotch Cookies
Crunchy and Flat

If you like crunchy cookies then these are your cookies. I like to make them ahead and freeze. They are always a great stand-by to pull out of the freezer for dessert.

Makes approximately 48 cookies
1 C (2 sticks) unsalted butter - softened
1 C +1 T sugar
1 C + 1 T light brown sugar
⅛ tsp kosher salt
1 tsp baking soda
1 tsp vanilla
2 large eggs
2 C + 4 T unbleached flour
1 C semi sweet chocolate chips
1 C butterscotch chips

Preheat oven to 350°. Parchment line a sheet pan.
Beat butter in a mixer until soft. Add sugars and beat until creamy. Add eggs and vanilla. Then add salt, baking soda and flour. Mix one minute. Add chips and mix 20 seconds or just until incorporated. Scoop out balls of dough with the large side of a melon baller. Roll in your hands to form a ball. Place on sheet pan about 2" apart.

Bake for 10 minutes. Remove and place on cooling racks.

These cookies freeze well.

Dairy Free Option:
Use Earth Balance® in place of the butter.

Gluten Free Option:
Omit the flour and replace it with 1½ C rice flour and ½ C + 4 T tapioca flour, 4 tsp xanthan gum.

Cooling or Baking Racks -
Oven-safe racks made of metal used for cooling or baking. The racks are elevated to allow airflow to cool cookies or other baked goods.

Oatmeal Cherry Cookies
With Pecans and Coconut

I like to make these ahead of time and freeze. They are always a great stand-by to pull out of the freezer last minute for dessert.

Makes approximately 40 cookies
1 C (2 sticks) unsalted butter - softened
1 C sugar
1 C brown sugar
2 eggs
2 tsp vanilla
3 C old fashioned oats
1½ C flour
1 tsp kosher salt
1 tsp baking soda
1 tsp ground cinnamon
1 C coconut flakes
1 C cherries - dried
1 C pecans - chopped

Preheat oven to 350°. Parchment line a sheet pan.
Beat butter in a mixer until soft. Add sugars and beat until creamy. Add all but the last 3 ingredients and mix well. Then add coconut, cherries and pecans. Scoop out balls of dough with the large side of a melon baller. Place on sheet pan, about 2" apart.

Bake 350° for 10 minutes. Remove and place on cooling racks.

These cookies freeze well.

> **Dairy Free Option:**
> Use Earth Balance® in place of the butter.
>
> **Gluten Free Option:**
> Omit the flour and replace it with 1 C rice flour and ½ C tapioca flour, 4 tsp xanthan gum.

> **Cooling or Baking Racks -**
> Oven-safe racks made of metal used for cooling or baking. The racks are elevated to allow airflow to cool cookies or other baked goods.

Gingerbread People
With Royal Icing

For the last 12 years I've done a Christmas cookie party for one of my favorite client's children and their friends. It's always been a wonderful experience seeing their creatively decorated cookies.

Makes approximately 48 cookies depending on cutter size
1 C (2 sticks) unsalted butter - softened
1¼ C dark brown sugar
2 eggs
½ C molasses
4 C flour – add more to get the texture soft, but not sticky
3 T ground ginger
¾ tsp ground cinnamon
¾ tsp baking soda
¼ tsp kosher salt

Dairy Free Option: Use Earth Balance® in place of the butter.

Preheat oven to 350°. Parchment line a sheet pan.
Beat the butter with the sugar in a mixer until creamy. Add eggs then molasses. Then add the rest of the ingredients. Refrigerate overnight or for a few hours. Roll out between two pieces of parchment paper. Cut with cookie cutters. Bake 10 minutes. Remove and place on cooling racks. Decorate with royal icing.

GF & DF

Cindy's Lemon Royal Icing
Since the scare with Salmonella, I started using dehydrated egg whites also listed as Meringue Powder. It has been pasteurized. You can find this online at King Arthur Flour® or in some specialty grocery stores.

¼ C dehydrated egg whites
¾ C + 2 T water
2 lemons - juiced
2 lbs powdered sugar

Whisk the egg whites, water and lemon juice in a mixer until stiff peaks form. Add powdered sugar and whisk until smooth.

Colored Icing
Royal icing - above
1 bottle red food coloring
1 bottle green food coloring

Split the icing into 3 portions - one for the white, one for green and one for red. The food coloring will make the icing thinner, so take care with consistency. Mix each color with a mixer in separate bowls. When color is blended, put into a Ziploc® bag. When ready to use, cut off a tiny tip at one end of the Ziploc® and use as a pastry bag for decorating.

Linzer Cookies
With Powdered Sugar and Raspberry Jam

I like to make these ahead of time, freeze, and then take out when I want to add the jam and serve. They look really pretty served on the same platter as the Bûchë de Noël, pg. 139.

Makes approximately 24 cookies
2 C (4 sticks) unsalted butter - softened
2 C powdered sugar
2 C ground almonds - (grind in a food processor)
2 tsp vanilla
4 C flour
1 to 2 T water, brandy or Chambord liqueur

Assembly
2 C powdered sugar to coat
1 jar raspberry jam for filling

Linzer Cookie Cutter Set -
You can get these at a kitchen shop like Williiams Sonoma® or online at King Arthur Flour®.

Parchment Paper -
I like to roll out my cookie dough between 2 full size sheets of parchment paper without flour. If you use flour, it adds to the dough, making the second roll out strange. Then the cookies aren't as pretty and taste heavier.

Preheat oven to 350°. Parchment line a sheet pan.
Beat sugar and butter in a mixer until creamy. Add almonds, vanilla and flour. Add water, brandy or liqueur 1 T at a time to thin the dough out if it's too crumbly. You want it moist enough to hold together. Roll out dough between 2 full sheets of parchment paper. Use a Linzer cookie cutter set and cut equal amounts of bases and tops with cut-out shapes. Bake for 10 minutes. Remove and place on cooling racks. Roll in powdered sugar to coat heavily.

These can be frozen at this point.

When ready to serve, take the base and dollop a ½ tsp of raspberry jam in the center. Then put the top piece on. Platter and serve.

Holiday Sugar Cookies
Chocolate Dipped or Royal Icing

I like to make these ahead of time, freeze, and then take out when I want to decorate. These cookies have been favorites at many Aspen Christmas parties I've catered.

Makes approximately 48 cookies depending on cutter size

1 C unsalted butter - softened
4 C flour
2 C sugar
½ tsp kosher salt
1 tsp baking powder
2 eggs
4 T brandy or Grand Marnier®
1 tsp vanilla

Dairy Free Option: Use Earth Balance® in place of the butter.

Preheat oven to 350°. Parchment line a sheet pan.
Beat sugar and butter in a mixer until creamy. Add the rest of the ingredients and mix well. Roll out the dough between 2 pieces of parchment paper. Cut with holiday cookie cutters. Bake for 10 minutes. Remove and place on cooling racks.

Chocolate Dipped and Sprinkles   GF

16 oz semi sweet chocolate
Sprinkles - holiday sprinkles, glitter, cinnamon drops, etc...

Melt the chocolate in double boiler. Dip the cookies and place on a parchment-lined sheet pan to set chocolate. Put sprinkles on while the chocolate is still warm. If you live in a cold climate you can speed up the setting process by putting the dipped cookies in a safe place outside until chocolate is firm. Make sure animals can't get to them. Chocolate is toxic to most animals.

Cindy's Lemon Royal Icing   GF & DF

Since the scare with Salmonella, I started using dehydrated egg whites, also listed as meringue powder. It has been pasteurized. You can find this online at King Arthur Flour® or in some specialty grocery stores.

¼ C dehydrated egg whites
¾ C + 2 T water
2 lemons - juiced
2 lbs powdered sugar

Whisk the egg whites, water and lemon juice in a mixer until stiff peaks form. Add powdered sugar and whisk until smooth.

You can also color the icing with whatever food colors you like. When color is blended, put into Ziploc® bag. When ready to use, cut off a tiny tip at one end of the bag and use as a pastry bag for decorating. Add sprinkles before the icing sets.

Bernice's Pecan Slices
With Coconut Flakes

These delicious 50's classic treats come from my former mother in-law Bernice, Chicago, Illinois. Bernice was the queen of baked goods.

Makes approximately 20 pieces

Crust
½ C (1 stick) unsalted butter - softened
1 C flour
1 T water

> **Dairy Free Option:**
> Use Earth Balance® in place of the butter.

Preheat oven to 350°.
Beat the butter and flour in a mixer. Add water. Put the crust into a greased 8" x 8" glass pan. It will need to be worked into the bottom of the pan with your fingers. Then press down with a measuring cup to firm it up.

Bake the crust 15–20 minutes.

Filling
2 eggs beaten
1½ C brown sugar
2 T flour
½ tsp baking powder
1 C coconut flakes
1 C pecans - chopped

Mix the filling ingredients in a mixer. Place on the crust in little dabs. Carefully spread the filling or the crust will break.

Bake 25 minutes longer.

Dust with powdered sugar. Cut into squares while still warm.

Option…can add 1 C chocolate chips to the top for the last 5 minutes of baking.

Aunt Libby's Bourbon balls
For Grown ups ONLY! A Southern Delight - with Wild Turkey

GF

Cary and I worked in the kitchen at Bonnies Restaurant in Aspen. She brought these as Christmas treats for the staff one season. Cary was kind enough to share these amazing holiday treats that were memorable and delicious! This recipe comes from her beloved Aunt Libby. They are a southern treat for the holidays. THEY DO CONTAIN ALCOHOL!

Makes approximately 100 bourbon balls
6 oz 100 proof bourbon (101 Wild Turkey®)
1½ C pecan pieces
8 C powdered sugar
1½ sticks butter
8 oz semi-sweet chocolate
1½ oz paraffin (optional)

Soak pecans overnight in the Wild Turkey, in an airtight container. Strain nuts.
Melt butter, add powdered sugar, then add strained nuts. Refrigerate for 1 hour. This will keep the mixture from being too sticky when you roll.

Melt chocolate and paraffin (if using) in a double boiler.

Gluten Free WARNING: Some experts say that the distillation process removes harmful gluten proteins from alcohol. Some experts advise using only alcohol made from non-gluten grain sources. Use your own judgement if you are allergic to gluten. Some alcohol distilleries might add caramel color which can contain gluten.

Using a melon baller, scoop mixture into little balls. Roll in your hands to form round balls. Use one to two toothpicks to stick into a ball. This will hold the ball while you dip and coat each ball in the chocolate/paraffin melted mix. Place on waxed paper to set. Freeze to harden.

Best if kept refrigerated until ready to serve.

Pecan Balls Rolled in Powder Sugar
Also Known as Mexican Wedding Cookies

I have an awesome client from New York who sends me a 2 gallon bag of fresh pecans after harvest. I make these cookies every year as Christmas treats made with some of his pecans.

Makes approximately 30 cookies
1 C (2 sticks) unsalted butter - softened
¼ C sugar
2 tsp vanilla
pinch of kosher salt
2 C flour
2 C pecans - chopped
2 C powdered sugar - to coat cookies

Dairy Free-Vegan Option:
Use Earth Balance® in place of the butter.

Gluten Free Option:
Omit the flour and replace it with 1¼ C rice flour, ¼ C potato starch, ½ C tapioca flour and 4 tsp xanthan gum.

Preheat oven to 350°. Parchment line a sheet pan.
Chop the pecans in a food processor. Set aside.
Beat the butter and sugar in a mixer until creamy. Add the vanilla, salt, flour and pecans, mix until incorporated. Refrigerate 30 minutes.

Scoop a ball with the large side of a melon baller and roll in your hands. Place on cookie sheet. Repeat until done.

Bake for 10-15 minutes until light golden brown. When slightly cooled, coat in powdered sugar. Cool completely on a cooling rack and toss in powdered sugar again to get a good coating.

These store in your refrigerator in an airtight container for at least a month and in the freezer for 6 months.

Chocolate Gluten Free Cookies
With Caramel Surprises

GF

This recipe is also really good without the caramel candy inside. It's a lot less sweet and makes it dairy free. If you can serve these warm out of the oven, you will certainly impress your guests. My chocolate-loving clients love these!

Makes approximately 24 cookies
10 T Earth Balance® - softened
1½ C dark brown sugar
1½ C sugar
2 large eggs
1½ tsp vanilla
½ tsp kosher salt
1½ tsp baking powder
⅔ C unsweetened cocoa powder
1 C rice flour
½ C tapioca flour
4 tsp xanthan gum
2 C powdered sugar
24 caramel candies or Rolos®

> **Dairy Free Option:**
> Omit the caramel or Rolos®. I prefer these cookies without the caramel.

> **Cooling or Baking Racks -**
> Oven-safe racks made of metal used for cooling or baking. The racks are elevated to allow airflow to cool cookies or other baked goods.

Preheat oven to 325°. Parchment line a sheet pan.

Beat Earth Balance® in a mixer until soft. Add sugars and beat until creamy. Add eggs and vanilla. Then add salt, baking powder, cocoa powder, rice flour, tapioca flour and xanthan gum, mix one minute.

Take about 1½ tablespoons of dough in your palm and add caramel candy or Rolo to the center. Fold dough over candy and roll into a ball. Toss into a bowl of powdered sugar and roll a couple of times to coat heavily. Place on sheet pan, about 2" apart. Bake for 10 minutes. The tops should begin to crack. Let cool 5 minutes on the sheet pan, then remove and place on a cooling rack until completely cooled.

Store in an airtight container or freeze for later.

Chocolate Peanut Butter Brownies
With a Chocolate Ganache

I have a client who loves the combination of chocolate and peanut butter. These do the job. Put a small scoop of vanilla ice cream on the side and seal the deal.

Makes approximately 48 brownies
8 oz unsweetened chocolate
2 C (4 sticks) unsalted butter - softened
4 C sugar
8 eggs
1 T vanilla
½ tsp kosher salt
2¼ C flour
1 C raw virginia peanuts or pecans chopped (optional)

Preheat oven to 320°. Grease and flour a large 13½ X 10 pan. I foil line the pan, spray with Pam® and coat with flour. This saves time on clean up and ease removing brownies from the pan.

Melt butter and chocolate in double boiler. Add sugar and mix well.
Beat eggs and vanilla in a mixer. While the mixer is running, add the melted chocolate/sugar mix. Add flour, salt, then nuts if using. Pour into greased and floured baking pan.

Bake at 320° for 1 hour. Take out and cool pan on cooling racks then lift foil to remove.

Peanut Butter Frosting
2 C powdered sugar
⅔ C peanut butter
4 to 5 T milk or whipping cream, or more to thin

Whisk all the ingredients in a mixer until a smooth spreadable consistency. When brownies are cooled, spread peanut butter frosting on top. Then finish with the chocolate ganache.

Chocolate Ganache
9.7 oz Scharffen Berger bittersweet dark chocolate bar
¾ C heavy whipping cream

Melt the chocolate in a double boiler. Remove from heat and whisk in the heavy whipping cream. Cool slightly and pour on top of the peanut butter frosted brownies. You can also top with caramelized peanuts pg. 146.

Lemon Bars
With a Shortbread Crust

Makes approximately 24 pieces

Shortbread Crust
1 C (2 sticks) unsalted butter - softened
½ C powdered sugar
½ tsp kosher salt
2 C flour
2 T water

> **Dairy Free:**
> Use Earth Balance® or coconut oil in place of butter.

Blend crust ingredients in a mixer, it will be crumbly. Take your hands and press into a greased 9 x 13 glass baking pan. Then use a measuring cup to flatten.
Bake at 350° for 15–20 minutes or until golden brown.

Lemon Curd Filling
4 eggs - beaten
2 C sugar
½ tsp baking powder
¼ C flour
4 lemons - zest and juice

Preheat oven to 350°.
Beat eggs and sugar in a mixer. Add the flour, then lemon juice and zest. Pour over baked crust. Bake for 20-25 minutes until filling is set. Cool.

Sprinkle with powdered sugar while still warm, then again after cooled.

Italian Biscotti - Chocolate Dipped
With Apricots, Cherries, Almonds & Anise

Makes approximately 48 cookies

1 C (2 sticks) unsalted butter - softened
2 C sugar
¼ C anise seeds
¼ C anisette liqueur
3 T whiskey
6 eggs
5½ C flour
1 T baking powder
2 C almonds - coarsely chopped
1 C apricots - coarsely chopped
½ C cherries - coarsely chopped

Dairy Free:
Use Earth Balance® or coconut oil in place of butter.

Preheat oven to 350°. Parchment line a sheet pan.
Beat sugar and butter in a mixer until creamy. Add the anise seeds, anisette and whisky. Beat in eggs. Add flour and baking powder, mix well. Add nuts and fruit, mix until incorporated. Cover and refrigerate 2–3 hrs

Separate dough into 4 to 5 balls, place on 2 parchment-lined cookie sheets. With your hands form and flatten into logs ½" high by 3" wide, and as long as your cookie sheet.

Bake for 20–30 minutes or until golden brown.

Remove from oven, let cool. Slice logs across in a slight diagonal about ½" to ¾" wide. Put back on cookie sheet and bake for 15 minutes more or until lightly toasted.

Remove and place on cooling racks. When cool, dip half of the cookie in semi sweet chocolate (below).

For Chocolate Dipping
16 oz semi sweet chocolate
Swedish Pearled Sugar (King Arthur Flour® - online) - to decorate

Melt chocolate in a double boiler. Dip the cookies halfway into melted chocolate and place on a parchment-lined sheet pan. Sprinkle pearled sugar onto chocolate while it's still warm. Let cookies set until chocolate is firm.

60's Holiday Egg Nog
Virgin or Boozy

GF

This is also really good virgin, without the alcohol. This recipe came from an aunt of mine from the 60's and the booze was tripled. I reduced the amount of alcohol considerably and it's still delicious. I got a great tip from my friend Dale one Christmas eve at a dinner party in Aspen, on how to make your egg nog thick and creamy. She suggested whipping the heavy cream and egg whites, then folding them into the rest of the egg nog mix.

Makes approximately 1¼ gallons

1 qt half-and-half
1 qt whipping cream
½ gallon whole milk
2½ C sugar
6 eggs - separated
¼ C brandy - optional
½ C rum - optional
4 oz bourbon or whiskey - optional (not GF)
nutmeg - whole, finely grated (ground, optional)

Separate eggs. In a large pitcher, beat yolks, add sugar, whole milk and half and half. Let meld overnight or at least 4 hours before serving. 1 hour before serving, whip the whipping cream just until it starts to thicken. Beat egg whites until stiff not dry. Fold the stiff egg whites and whipped cream to the egg nog base. Serve as a virgin egg nog or add booze.

I usually have two pitchers at the party, one with alcohol and one virgin. You can always add booze to the virgin one if needed.

Gluten Free WARNING: Some experts say that the distillation process removes harmful gluten proteins from alcohol. Some experts advise using only alcohol made from non-gluten grain sources. Use your own judgement if you are allergic to gluten. Some alcohol distilleries might add caramel color which can contain gluten.
If you are sensitive to gluten, omit the bourbon/whiskey.

Whole Nutmeg - To finely grate whole nutmeg use a nutmeg grater. They are easy to find online. Freshly grated nutmeg goes a long way and is worth the effort.

Collections from an Aspen Chef
Favorite recipes with options to accommodate your dietary preferences

GF = Gluten Free ~ DF = Dairy Free ~ VG = Vegan ~ ❄ = Freezes Well

Collections from an Aspen Chef

Favorite recipes with options to accommodate your dietary preferences

Breakfast Yummies:

Cheri's Banana Nut Bread	170
Kinch's Granola Bars	171
Crunchy Granola	171
Blueberry/Banana Pancakes	172
Corn Grit Waffles	173
Blueberry Muffins	174
Pineapple Banana Oatbran Muffins	175
Carrot/Pineapple Muffins w/Vegan Cream Cheese Frosting	176
Sally's Famous Scone Balls	177
Eggs Benedict	178
Quiche & Frittatas-Spanish Omelets	179

Cheri's Banana Nut Bread
Delicious with or without nuts

Cheri and I worked at Bonnies restaurant together. She was kind enough to share this delicious recipe. Her banana nut bread is an Aspen favorite.

Makes 1 loaf pan or 4 mini loaves

3 ripe bananas
2 eggs
1¾ C flour
1 C sugar
1 C chopped walnuts
½ C canola oil
¼ C + 1 T buttermilk
1 tsp baking soda
1 tsp vanilla
½ tsp kosher salt

Dairy Free Option:
Use coconut milk in the carton or soy milk in place of the buttermilk.

Nut Free Option:
Don't use walnuts or any nuts.

Mix all the ingredients in a mixer. Refrigerate overnight for better flavor.
Preheat oven to 350°. Grease and flour one 9"x 5" loaf pan or 4 mini loaf pans.
Bake 1 hour for a full loaf. If using the mini loaf pans, check at 25 minutes and rotate pans. Then bake another 20 - 25 minutes.

This freezes well.

Kinch's Granola Bars
And Crunchy Granola

❄ GF, DF & VG

Kinch is a cross-county ski racer in the winter and an extreme croquet player in the summer. These are great snacks to take along for outdoor activities. Thanks Kinch for sharing!

Kinch's Granola Bars - *Makes one 11"x14.5" pan of bars*
1 lb granola
5 oz crisped rice cereal (check label for GF)
1 (21 oz) jar brown rice syrup (easier to mix if warmed)
1 (24 oz) jar peanut butter (easier to mix if warmed)
1½ lbs dried cherry berry mix (Cherryland® is best)
1 lb mini dark chocolate chips (look for dairy free)
2 tsp cinnamon (or more to taste)

In a very large bowl mix dry ingredients with a spatula. Fold wet into dry until uniform (you need strong arms). Put into a turkey roaster pan 11" x 14.5". Pack it down with a rolling pin. Cover with foil, then into a plastic bag. Let set overnight. Cut into bars - enjoy!

Crunchy Granola - *Makes one sheet pan of granola*
Preheat oven to 375° for 15 minutes.

Dry Mix
7½ C oats - GF (old fashion, not quick)
1½ C oat bran
1 C coconut - flaked
½ C ground flax seed meal
1 C sunflower seeds
1 C slivered almonds
1 tsp kosher salt
1½ C dried tart cherries - add after baking
1 C chopped dates - add after baking
1 C chopped apricots - add after baking

> **Gluten Free Oats:** Check the label, some oats are processed in a facility with wheat. If someone has Celiac disease, you really need to be careful.

Wet Mix - Mix into a separate container to pour as one combined mix
3 T orange juice concentrate
1 tsp vanilla
1 C brown sugar
¾ C + 2 T canola oil

On a parchment-lined sheet pan combine the dry ingredients, except cherries, dates and apricots. Pour on the wet mixture. Toss really well using your hands to coat the dry with the wet. Put into preheated oven for 7 minutes, take out and mix. Bake another 7 minutes, take out and mix. Return to oven. **Turn oven off, don't open the oven door!** Leave in overnight. In the morning, take out and add cherries, dates and apricots. Mix well and store in airtight containers or freeze.

Blueberrry Banana Pancakes
With Blackberry Syrup

GF

Makes about 25 to 30 pancakes

Cooking Stage
2 bananas - ⅛" sliced
1 half pint of blueberries

Batter
4 C rolled oats - GF
1 quart buttermilk
4 eggs
½ C (1 stick) melted butter
½ C sugar
¾ C rice flour
¼ C potato starch
2 T tapioca flour
½ tsp xanthan gum
2 tsp baking soda
2 tsp baking powder
¼ tsp kosher salt
1½ - 2 C whole milk (add later to thin)

> **Dairy Free Option:**
> I prefer to use So Delicious® Coconut Milk in place of the buttermilk and milk, and coconut oil in place of the butter.
>
> **Wheat Option:**
> If you can tolerate gluten, use 1 C flour in place of the rice flour, potato starch, tapioca flour & xanthan gum.

In a big pitcher combine oats and buttermilk. Stir well. Add eggs and melted butter then follow with the rest of the ingredients, except for the whole milk (save for thinning batter).

Let meld for at least 2 hours or overnight. Add the remaining 1½ - 2 C milk to thin to the consistency you like. I prefer my batter thin, this will keep for 5 days in your refrigerator.

Heat your skillet or griddle on medium heat, spray with Pam®.

Have banana slices and blueberries ready to add to pancakes.

Add a ladlefull of pancake batter to the hot griddle and immediately add about 8 blueberries and 6 slices of bananas. When browned on the bottom - flip. Cook until pancakes are done. Sprinkle with powdered sugar and serve with Blackberry Maple Syrup (below).

Blackberry Maple Syrup   ❄ GF, DF & VG
3 pints blackberries or 1 package frozen blackberries - thawed
½ C maple syrup
½ lemon - juiced

Bring to a boil, then simmer for 5-10 minutes. Will hold in the fridge for 5 days.

Corn Grit Waffles
Gluten and Dairy Free

❄ **GF & DF**

Makes about 10 waffles
1 C cornmeal
½ C rice flour
¼ C potato starch
2 tsp baking powder
½ tsp kosher salt
3 T sugar
4 T coconut oil - softened
3 egg yolks
1⅓ C coconut milk, in carton pg. 10
3 egg whites - whip to stiff peaks

In a separate bowl whip egg whites stiff, but not dry.
Mix coconut oil and dry ingredients in another bowl and cut with a pastry cutter. Add egg yolks and coconut milk. Mix with a plastic spatula. Fold in whipped egg whites.

Heat your waffle iron and spray with Pam®.

Makes about 6 - 8 waffles depending on the iron.

I like to serve these with a good berry jam and or maple syrup.

I usually make the whole batch and freeze extra waffles between parchment paper. Bring out to toast and eat. They hold really well in the freezer!

Blueberry Muffins
Or Strawberry Peach Instead

These blueberry muffins were a hit with my favorite breakfast clients in Aspen for nearly 12 years. I had to hide a few muffins for the late risers.

Makes about 16 small muffins or 8 large muffins

3 C flour
1 T baking powder
½ tsp baking soda
½ tsp kosher salt
2 ripe bananas (optional)
10 T unsalted butter - softened
1 C sugar (or ½ C Truvia if you're watching your sugar)
2 large eggs
1½ C plain yogurt
2 tsp grated lemon zest
1½ C frozen blueberries (or strawberries and peaches)

Dairy Free Option:
Use coconut yogurt in place of plain yogurt, and coconut oil or Earth Balance®, in place of butter.

Gluten Free Option:
Replace flour with
2 C rice flour
½ C potato starch
¼ C cornstarch
¼ C tapioca flour
2 tsp xanthan gum

Preheat oven to 325°.
Mix dry ingredients, except sugar, in a separate bowl. Set aside.
Beat butter and sugar in a mixer on medium speed until light and fluffy. Add eggs. Beat in half of dry ingredients, then half of yogurt, alternating until the batter is incorporated. Don't overmix. Add blueberries and mix another 10 seconds.

Spray muffin pan with Pam®. Fill with batter (a little over the lip). There is usually enough for 8 large muffins or 16 small muffins. Bake 25 minutes, rotate. Continue baking until brown, another 20 minutes. Oven calibrations and altitude will affect the way your muffins bake. Insert toothpick into center of muffin, if it comes out clean, they are done.

Optional - before you put the muffins in the oven, sprinkle with sugar or a cinnamon sugar mix, about 2 tsp on top of each muffin.

Pineapple Banana Oatbran Muffins ❄ GF & DF
Dairy Free and Gluten Free

Makes about 18 medium muffins or 9 large muffins

1 C coconut oil
½ C brown sugar
½ C sugar
4 ripe bananas
2 eggs
2 tsp baking powder
½ tsp baking soda
½ tsp salt
2 tsp xanthan gum
1 C rice flour
½ C tapioca flour
½ C potato starch
2 C oatbran cereal, or granola - GF
½ C pineapple - chopped
½ C blueberries – fresh or frozen
½ C walnuts or pecans (optional) - chopped

Freezing Bananas-
Put bananas that are on the edge of going bad into the freezer, whole with skin on. When you need bananas for a baking recipe take out of the freezer, thaw, remove peel and they are ready to use.

Preheat oven to 350°.
Beat coconut oil, sugar and bananas in a mixer on medium speed. Add eggs and combine. Add dry ingredients and mix until batter is incorporated. Then add oatbran cereal, pineapple, blueberries and nuts. Mix until blended.

Spray muffin pan with Pam®. Fill cups with batter (a little over the lip). Bake 25-35 minutes. Oven calibrations and altitude will affect the way your muffins bake. Insert toothpick into center of muffin, if it comes out clean, they are done.

Carrot Pineapple Flax Muffins
With a Vegan Cream Cheese Frosting

❄ GF, DF & VG

Makes about 16 small muffins or 10 large muffins

2½ C rice flour
½ C potato starch
¾ C almond flour or meal
¼ C ground flaxmeal
2 tsp xanthan gum
1 T baking powder
½ tsp baking soda
½ tsp kosher salt
10 T softened coconut oil or Earth Balance®
1 C sugar (or ½ C Truvia® if you are cutting your sugar intake)
1 ripe banana
1½ C grated carrots
1 C chopped pineapple
½ C chopped walnuts or pecans (optional)
1½ C coconut yogurt or 1 (15 oz) can 100% pumpkin purée
½ C frozen blueberries

Nut Free Option:
Replace the rice flour, potato starch and almond meal with:
2½ C rice flour
½ C potato starch
½ C cornstarch
¼ C tapioca flour
Leave out walnuts and pecans.

Yogurt Free Option:
100% pumpkin purée is a great substitute for yogurt. It adds the same amount of moisture to your mufffin mix.

Preheat oven to 325°.
Mix dry ingredients, except sugar, in a separate bowl. Set aside.
Beat coconut oil or Earth Balance®, sugar and bananas in a mixer on medium speed. Add dry ingredients, then yogurt or pure pumpkin. Mix batter until incorporated. Then add carrots, pineapple and nuts. Mix until blended. Lastly, add the blueberries and mix for 10 seconds.

Spray muffin pan with Pam®. Fill cups with batter (a little over the lip). There is usually enough for 8 large muffins or 16 small muffins. Bake 25 minutes, rotate. Continue cooking until brown, another 20 minutes. Oven calibrations and altitude will affect the way your muffins bake. Insert toothpick into center of muffin, if it comes out clean, they are done.
Optional - before you put the muffins in the oven, sprinkle with sugar or a cinnamon sugar mix, about 1 tsp on each muffin.

Vegan Cream Cheese Frosting
1 stick Earth Balance®
1 (8 oz) container Tofutti® Better Than Cream Cheese - softened
1 lb powdered sugar
1 tsp vanilla

In a mixer, whip the Earth Balance®, Toffuti® cream cheese and vanilla. Add powdered sugar and whip until smooth. If there is leftover frosting, it freezes well.

Sally's Famous Scone Balls
With Fresh Berries

Sally has gladly shared one of her Texas family favorites. I think Sally puts the batter into a 9"round pan, or forms batter into football shapes, instead of forming balls.

Makes about 24 scone balls

3 C unbleached flour
½ C sugar
1 T baking powder
½ tsp kosher salt
½ C + 2T buttermilk
1 egg
1½ sticks unsalted butter - chilled and cubed into ½" pieces
4 oz cream cheese - chilled and cubed into ½" pieces
1 pint each of raspberries, blueberries and blackberries

Preheat oven to 350°. Line a baking sheet with parchment paper. Mix dry ingredients in a mixer. Add egg, buttermilk, mix. Then add chilled butter and cream cheese. Mix until combined. Take 2 T of batter into your palm and add berries, folding them in one at a time, encasing berries. Add more dough to cover berries.

Bake 15–20 minutes until golden brown.

Dairy Free Option:
Use Earth Balance® for the butter and Toffuti® Better Than Cream Cheese in place of the cream cheese, use coconut milk in the carton in place of the buttermilk.

Vegan Option:
Follow the dairy free options and replace egg with 1 T potato starch and 1 T tapioca flour.

Eggs Benedict
With Asparagus, Spinach & Tomatoes

One of my favorite famlies would request Eggs Benedict and waffles for dinner.

Serves 6
You will need an egg poacher and a blender for this recipe.

Hollandaise Sauce - *blender method*   **GF**
1 C butter (2 sticks) - melted
6 egg yolks
3 lemons - juiced
pinch of cayenne
½ tsp kosher salt
fresh ground black pepper to taste

Heat the butter in a saucepan and hold on low until you are ready to make the Hollandaise sauce. Meanwhile, add the egg yolks, lemon juice, cayenne, salt and pepper to a blender. Put the lid on the blender and hold until ready to add butter and serve. Remove the clear ingredient cup, leaving an open hole in the lid to pour melted butter through. Then, with the blender running, drizzle in the melted butter and blend until mixed, about 30 seconds.

Eggs Benedict
1 pkg sourdough English muffins (I prefer Bay's®)
1 ½ dozen eggs
12 slices Canadian bacon
2 bunches asparagus
1 (1 lb) bag fresh spinach
6 campari tomatoes or farmers market heirlooms

> **Gluten Free Option:** Use gluten free English muffins. Found in the freezer section of your grocery store.

Blanch asparagus, drain and keep warm in pan on stove. Steam the spinach until limp. Slice the tomatoes. Toast the English muffins and keep warm in a 200° oven. Sauté the Canadian bacon and hold in the oven. You can do this half an hour before serving. Poach eggs for 5-10 minutes depending on how you like them.

Assembly - For each plate - Place 6 spears of asparagus with tips towards the center of the plate, topped with a mound of wilted spinach at the base. Add 3 slices of tomatoes. Put two English muffins on either side of the veggies and top each English muffin with two pieces of Canadian bacon. Finally add a poached egg to each English muffin. Drizzle a generous amount of Hollandaise sauce on top. Serve at once.

Quiche & Frittata - Spanish Omelet
Easy Breakfast Buffet Dishes

Olive Oil Pie Crust - *Serves 8*
1½ C flour
½ C olive oil or canola oil (canola oil is flavorless)
½ tsp kosher salt
¼ C water or milk
¼ tsp baking powder

In a mixer add all the ingredients and combine. Place in a 9" pie dish, press down with your fingers then a measuring cup to form crust.

Filling
3 eggs - beaten
2 C heavy cream
1 C Gruyère cheese - grated
8 slices bacon - cooked and crumbled
2 big handfuls of fresh spinach
2 sliced Campari tomatoes or fresh farmers market Early Girls
6 asparagus spears - trim bottom off
pinch of ground nutmeg
S & P

Gluten Free Option: Omit the flour and replace it with 1 C rice flour and ½ C tapioca flour, 4 tsp xanthan gum. The texture will be different, but the flavor will be great. Follow the same instructions.

Preheat oven to 350°. Beat eggs. Add heavy cream, then the rest of the ingredients. Pour filling into pie crust, except tomatoes and asparagus. Top with sliced tomatoes and asparagus spears. Bake at 350° for 35-40 minutes, until top is golden brown.

Frittata - *Serves 8* ❄ GF
3 T olive oil
6 slices prosciutto - sliced into thin strips (or leftover ham)
7 mushrooms - cleaned and sliced thin
1 zucchini - sliced thin
3 red potatoes - parboiled until fork tender, sliced thin
2 tsp fresh marjoram or basil - loosely chopped
3 green onions - cleaned and chopped
1 lb spinach - steam, until limp
6 eggs - beaten
1 C whole milk
1 C Gruyère cheese - grated
S & P

Dairy Free Option: Omit the whole milk and use coconut milk in the carton. Also omit the Gruyère cheese, its still tasty.

Preheat oven to 350°. Heat 8" cast iron skillet on stovetop. Add olive oil, sauté prosciutto, mushrooms, and zucchini, sauté 5 minutes. Add potatoes and fresh marjoram or basil, green onions and spinach. Mix. In a separate bowl, beat eggs, milk and cheese, S & P to taste and add to the skillet. Don't stir. Bake 45 minutes to 1 hour, until the top is golden brown. Remove from oven. Run a knife or long spatula under the fritta to loosen it up. Put a plate over the skillet, invert pan and flip onto the plate. Cut into slices and serve.

Collections from an Aspen Chef ~ Cindy Rogers

Collections from an Aspen Chef
Favorite recipes with options to accommodate your dietary preferences

Collections from an Aspen Chef
Favorite recipes with options to accommodate your dietary preferences

Glossary

Abbreviations & Symbols -
DF - Dairy Free – eating dairy free means refraining from dairy products. A dairy product is a food produced from the milk of lactating mammals.
EGGS are NOT dairy!
GF - Gluten Free – A gluten-free diet is a diet that excludes gluten, a protein composite found in wheat and related grains, including barley and rye. Gluten causes health problems in those who suffer from celiac disease and cases of wheat allergies.
VG - Vegan – dietary vegans refrain from consuming animal products, not only meat but also eggs, dairy products and other animal-derived substances. Eating nothing that once had a face or a pulse.
❄ – **Freezes** really well.

Glossary -
Al Dente – slightly underdone with a chewy consistency.
Au Jus – natural pan juices that occur when roasting meat.
Aioli – a mayonnaise flavored with garlic, and other ingredients. Used as a dip or sauce.
Bamboo Steamer - a layered steamer used in this book for cooking pork purses.
Beat – use a spoon, fork, whisk, rotary, or electric beater to introduce air throughout any food mixture. Stir in rapid, regular, round-and-round or over-and-under strokes with a spoon or beater until mixture is smooth and creamy.
Blacken – coat fish or meat with seasoning and quickly sear in a very hot skillet, thereby producing meat that is black on the outside but tender on the inside.
Blanch – to immerse food in boiling water for a minute or so, then immediately drain and rinse in cold water or ice.
Bread Crumbs – fresh vs. baked. I like to use a French loaf, tear into pieces and pulse in the food processor until fine crumbs. At this point they can be used fresh as is. For baked bread crumbs, toast on a sheet pan in a 350° oven until golden brown.
Brine – a solution of salt and water.
Brown – to cook food quickly in a preheated oven, broiler or hot skillet to "brown" the outside and seal in the juices.
Caramelize – to slowly dissolve sugar in water or butter, then continue cooking on low until it turns caramel brown.
Casein and Whey Allergies – casein is a protein in milk. Another milk protein associated with food allergies is whey. Some people are allergic to both. It is much different from lactose intolerant which is an intolerance to the sugar found in milk.
Chermoula Sauce – a zesty Moroccan marinade and sauce used to flavor and garnish meats, fish, seafood and veggies.

Collections from an Aspen Chef
Favorite recipes with options to accommodate your dietary preferences

Chiffonade – very finely shredded or thinly sliced herb or vegetable leaves. Layer a stack of leaves, roll up and slice on the diagonal to get a fine shred.
Chinois – a conical sieve with very fine mesh.
Chop – to cut food into non-uniform pieces, which can range from small (finely chop), to large (coarsely chop). Loosely chop refers to leafy herbs and veggies.
Cooling or Baking Racks – racks made of metal for cooling baked cookies and other foods. Also used for elevating fried chicken when baking.
Coulis Sauce – a form of thick sauce made from puréed and strained fruits.
Crostini – small pieces of toasted or fried bread served with a topping as an appetizer.
Cube – to cut food into cube-shape pieces, ranging in size from ¼ inch to 1 inch.
Cuisinart®- a food processor similar to a blender only it has interchangeable blades and discs, instead of a fixed blade. Needs little or no liquid to operate.
Curd – a fruit curd is a dessert spread. Made with eggs, sugar and citrus fruit, such as lemon, lime, orange or tangerine.
Deglaze – a cooking technique using liquid to remove and dissolve browned food residue from the bottom of a pan. The browned bits are called *fond* (french for "base" or "foundation"); and is used to create delicious sauces, soups and gravies.
Dice – to cut into fine, small, medium or large pieces, ranging from ⅛ inch – 1 inch.
Double Boiler – a pan half-full of water with a glass or metal bowl that sits tightly on top to capture the heat and gently warm delicate ingredients.
Dry Rub – any mixture of ground spices that is made for the purpose of being rubbed on raw food before the food is cooked.
Dutch Oven – a thick-walled cooking pot (usually cast iron but also ceramic and clay) with a tight fitting lid.
Emulsify – to mix two or more immiscible liquids together to form an emulsion.
Fond – the browned bits of meat left in a pan after browning meat.
Fork Tender – A method to check if vegetables are done. Use a fork to insert into a vegetable, if the vegetables are soft and break apart they are done.
French Trim – to prepare a rack of lamb so the bone is protruding and excess fat is removed.
Frosting or Icing – a sweet, often creamy glaze made of sugar and a liquid, such as water or milk that is often enriched with ingredients like butter, egg whites, cream cheese or flavorings.
Ganache – a glaze, icing, sauce or filling for pastries and desserts. It is made from chocolate and cream.
Galette – an open face pie with the fruit exposed, with a freeform crust around the edges.
Glaze – a liquid used to form a coating on food.
Grate – to change a solid food to fine (finely grate) or medium shreds (grate) by

Collections from an Aspen Chef
Favorite recipes with options to accommodate your dietary preferences

rubbing it against a hand grater or placing it in a food processor.

Gravy – a sauce made from the juices that run naturally during cooking often thickened with flour, corn starch or arrowroot. Sometimes a pre-made stock is used along with natural juices.

Grill – to cook on a rack over very hot coals or gas grill.

Immersion blender – a kitchen appliance used to blend ingredients or purée food in the container in which they are prepared.

Julienne – to cut fresh vegetables or other foods into thin matchstick size strips of uniform length.

KitchenAid® - a stand-up mixer with a detachable paddle, whisk and bread hook - serves all your baking needs.

Macerate – to cover fruits with a liquid, often a liqueur or lemon juice and sugar, or just sugar. It needs to rest at least one hour until the flavors have melded and the fruit has softened.

Marinate – to tenderize and flavor food by placing it in a seasoned liquid. A marinade is usually composed of some combination of vinegar, lemon juice, wine, oil, herbs and/or spices.

Mark – (grill) a mark that is made on meats, fish, shellfish or vegetables when they are placed on a hot grill. To make a mark, heat grill to medium high. Place food on the hot rack for the specified time according to the recipe, then flip to mark the other side.

Mélange – mixture, assortment, medley or variety.

Medley – an assortment, mixture, mélange or variety.

Meringue - egg whites beaten stiffly with sugar.

Mince – to cut or chop into very fine pieces, no larger than $\frac{1}{8}$ inch square.

Paste – to purée into a fine paste.

Pâte Sucrée – a sweet dough.

Peel and De-vein Shrimp – to peel the shell off and remove the intestinal tract of a shrimp. Remove shells from shrimp, make a slit lengthwise on the outermost curve with a knife and remove the intestinal tract. Rinse under cold water.

Pie Weights – small ceramic or metal balls used in naked pie shells to prevent blistering and shrinking during pre-baking, (before adding the filling).

Pit – to remove the pits from fruit. Cherries have a special pitter that is used.

Pesto – a sauce originating in Genoa on the Ligurian coast of northern Italy. It traditionally consists of crushed garlic, basil, pine nuts, olive oil and Parmigiana-Reggiano. In this cookbook, pesto refers to a sauce of minced herbs, garlic, olive oil, citrus and sometimes nuts and or Parmigiana-Reggiano.

Plastic Storage Containers – use food-safe brands like Tupperware® or Rubbermaid®. Always look for the BPA free label on the packaging.

Pressure Cook – the process of cooking food, using water or other cooking liquid, in an

Collections from an Aspen Chef
Favorite recipes with options to accommodate your dietary preferences

airtight sealed vessel, known as a pressure cooker. Steam is trapped in the airtight vessel increasing the internal pressure and temperatures. After use, the pressure is slowly released so the vessel can be safely opened.
Pulse – the setting on your food processor that allows you to control your chop time.
Purée – to mash solid food or pass it through a food mill or food processor until it is smooth.
Ramekin – individual baking dish.
Reduce or Reduction Sauce – to thicken or concentrate a sauce by boiling down, which lessens the volume and intensifies the flavor.
Remoulade – a homemade mayonnaise sauce with the addition of herbs, veggies and spices. Used as an accompaniment to meat, fish and shellfish.
Roulade – a French term that comes from the word "rouler" meaning to roll.
Royal Icing – is the hard white icing made from beaten egg whites, powdered sugar and sometimes lemon juice.
Roux – the paste which is the basis of most white sauce, cream sauces, and gravies. It is made by blending melted fat and flour then cooking and browning which to adds to the flavor and removes the flour taste.
Sauté – to cook food in a pan containing a small amount of fat until lightly browned.
Scald – to quickly heat liquid to just below the boiling point.
Sear – to brown the surface of food, usually meat, by exposing it to high heat for a comparatively short time.
Shred – to tear or cut into long thin pieces.
Simmer – to slowly cook liquid alone or along with other ingredients over low heat, never boiling.
Silverskin – a white and slivery connective tissue surrounding various muscles in animals. It doesn't break down in cooking and is tough and chewy; so it's best to remove before cooking.
Skewer – long pin of metal or wood on which food is held while cooking.
Stemmed – to remove stems from herbs or leafy vegetables.
Stock – a long simmering, well flavored broth made from meat, poultry, fish or vegetables with the addition of herbs and spices. Strain before using.
Strain – to remove solids from liquids by pouring through a colander or sieve.
Sweat – usually refers to using salt to sweat the bitterness out of your eggplant or cucumber.
Tapenade – a dish consisting of pureed or finely chopped olives, capers, anchovies and olive oil.
Temper – to moderate and balance a cooking ingredient before gradually adding it to a hot ingredient, or vice versa, so as to avoid separation and curdling.
Toss – to quickly and gently mix ingredients with your hands, tongs or spoons.

Collections from an Aspen Chef
Favorite recipes with options to accommodate your dietary preferences

Toast Points – flattened pieces of bread, cut into shapes, brushed with olive oil and toasted in the oven. Used for all kinds of appetizers or hors d'oeuvres.

Vinaigrette – a dressing made from a mixture of vinegar, oils, salt and pepper. Mustard, garlic, shallots, anchovies or egg can also be added. Use as dressing for salads or other cold dishes.

Whip – to beat rapidly, either by hand or with an electric mixer, to add air and increase volume.

Whisk - a looped wire kitchen utensil attached to a handle used to mix or "whisk" sauces, dressings, eggs, and other liquid ingredients with a swift, circular motion.

Zest – to remove in thin strips or finely-grate the outermost colored peel or zest of citrus fruits. Be careful not to incorporate the bitter white pith that lies just beneath the surface of the peel.

Collections from an Aspen Chef
Favorite recipes with options to accommodate your dietary preferences

Index

A
Ahi Blackened, 93
al dente, 91, 92, 181
Appetizers: See Table of Contents, 18-31
Apple Pie, 130
Apple Tarte Tartin, 128
arrowroot, 131
Arugula, Watercress Salad, Lee's, 40
Asian Baby Back Ribs, 120
Asian Glazed Lamb Chops, 112
Asparagus, Goat Cheese & Prosciutto Rolls, 26
Asparagus, Roasted, 75
Au Jus, 118, 181
Aunt Libby's Bourbon Balls, 161

B
Baby Back Ribs, Asian Glazed, 120
Baked Potato Fries, 76
Baked Tortilla Strips, 52
Balsamic Dressing, 37
Banana Nut Bread, Cheri's, 170
Banana Pineapple Oatbran Muffins, 175
Bananas Foster, 142
Basic Pie Crust, 129, 130
Beef:
    Beef Bourguignon Soup, 49
    Beef Chili, Dad's, 50
    Beef Curry, Linda's dry, 114
    Beef Satés, 18
    Beef Stroganoff, 119
    Beef Tenderloin, Grilled, 116
    Blackened Steak, 93
    Filet Mignon, 117
    Prime Rib, 118,
    Steak au Poivre, 115
Better Than Bouillon, Organic Chicken Base, 10
Better Than Bouillon, Vegetable Base, 10
Biscotti, Italian, Chocolate Dipped, 166
Black Olive Tapenade Salad Dressing, 35
Black Olive Tapenade, 35
blacken, 181
Blackened Steak or Ahi, 93
Blackening Seasoning Mix – Cajun, 93
blanch, 181
blender, 14

Blueberry Banana Pancakes, 172
Blueberry Cobbler, 133
Blueberry Muffins,174
Bourbon Baked Beans, 69
Bourbon Balls, Aunt Libby's, 161
Bragg, Yellow Miso Vinaigrette, 44
Bread & Butter Pickles, 96
bread crumbs, 89, 181
Breakfast Yummies, 170-179
brine, 181
Brine, Will's Turkey, 104
brown, 181
Brownies, Chocolate Peanut Butter, 164
Brussels Sprout, Kale Salad, 34
Brussels Sprouts, Roasted, 66
Bûche de Noël, Yule Log Cake, 139
Butterflied Leg of Lamb, 111
Buttermilk Biscuits, Gluten Free, 80

C
Caesar Salad Dressing, 42
Caesar Salad, 42
Cajun Blackening Seasoning, 93
Cajun Dipping Sauce, 24
Cakes:
    Bûche de Noël, Yule Log Cake, 139
    Chocolate Eruptions, 137
    Chocolate Layered Mousse Cake, 136
    Grandmas Classic Cheesecake, 141
    Lemon Cake w/Lemon Curd & Seven Minute Icing, 146
    Lemon Pudding Cakes, 148
    Coconut Mini Loaf Cakes, 135
    Vegan Cheesecake, 140
Candied Lemon Zest, 145
Candied Cashews, 57
Candied Peanuts, 150
Canned Paonia Peaches, 99
caramelize, 181
Caramelized Onions, 54, 73
Caramelized Onion Soup, 56
Caramelized Pecans, 40
Caramelized Walnuts, 41
Carrot Ginger Soup, Puréed, 57
Carrot Pineapple Flax Muffins, 176
casein allergies, 89, 181

Collections from an Aspen Chef
Favorite recipes with options to accommodate your dietary preferences

Cashew Lemon Vinaigrette, 34
cast iron skillets & Dutch oven, 14
Cauliflower, Roasted, 75
Charra Beans, 70
Cheese Cake, Classic, 141
Cheese Cake, Vegan, 140
Cheri's Banana Nut Bread, 170
Chermoula Sauce, 38
Cherry Pie, Sour, 129
Cherry Port Vinaigrette, 41
Cherry Preserves, Sour, 100
Chicken:
    Chicken & Red Chili Soup, 52
    Chicken Indian Curry, 105
    Chicken Marinade, 39
    Chicken Milanese, 37
    Chicken Stock, Homemade, 53
    Chicken Dumpling Soup, 53
    Chicken Satés, 19
    Chicken Under a Brick, 107
    Fried Chicken, 110
    Hillbilly Chicken, 109
    Shredded Chicken, 85
chiffonade, 182
Chili Aioli Sauce, spicy, 20
Chili, Dad's, 50
Chili, Di Baby's, 54
chinois, 181
Chipotle Glazed Salmon, 124
Chocolate Chip Butterscotch Cookies, 155
Chocolate Cookies with Caramel, Gluten Free, 163
Chocolate Eruptions, 137
Chocolate Frosting, 136
Chocolate Ganache, 139, 164, 182
Chocolate Layered Mousse Cake, 136
Chocolate Mousse, 136
Chocolate Mousse, Vegan, 134
Chocolate Peanut Butter Brownies, 164
Chocolate Peanut Butter Torte, 150
Chocolate Truffles, 137
chop, 182
Chunky Gazpacho, 62
Cilantro Vinaigrette, 78
cleaning leeks, 59
coconut milk in a can, 10
coconut milk in a carton, 10
Coconut Mini Loaf Cakes, 135
Coconut Oil, LouAna® & Spectrum®, 10
Cookies: See Table of Contents, 154-166
cooking temperatures, 13

Coq au Vin, 108
Corn Grit Waffle's, 173
Corn Salad, Southwestern, 78
Cornbread, Holiday Stuffing, 68
Cornbread, Mrs. B's Skillet, 68
Cornbread, Southwestern, 67
coulis sauce, 182
Crab Cakes, Southwestern, 20
Cream Cheese Frosting, Vegan, 131
Creamy Polenta, 74
Creole Grilled Shrimp, 24
Creole Mustard Sauce, 23
Crostini, 31, 56, 182
Croutons, 42
Crust, Pie:
    Basic Pie Crust, 129, 130
    Olive Oil Pie Crust, 179
    Sweet Pie Crust, 128
Cuban Braised Pork, 122
cube, 182
Cuisinart®, 14, 182
Cumin Crusted Pork Tenderloin, 121
curd, 182
Curry:
    Chicken Indian Curry, 105
    Linda's Dry Beef Curry, 114
    Thai Red Chile Curry, 106

D

Dad's Beef Chili, 50
Danish Blue Cheese Dressing, 43
deglaze, 118, 182
Desserts, 128-151
DF, 181
Di Baby's Vegan Chili, 54
dice, 182
Dijon Honey Vinaigrette, 40
double boiler, 182
dry rub, 114, 182
Duck and Shrimp Spring Rolls, 27
Dumplings, 53
Dutch oven, 182
Dutch Star Spice Cookies, 154

E

Earth Balance®, Shortening and Buttery Spread, 10
Egg Nog, 167

Collections from an Aspen Chef
Favorite recipes with options to accommodate your dietary preferences

Eggs Benedict, 178
Enchilada Sauce, 88
Endive Salad, Bonnie's Inspired, 41

F

Fall Kabocha Squash Soup, 48
Farrotto, 71
Fig Balsamic Dressing, 45
Fig Crostini with Brie and Bacon, 31
Fig Reduction Sauce, 31
Figs Prosciutto Goat Cheese 31
Filé Gumbo, 55
Filet Mignon, 117
food processor, 14
FoodSaver®, 182
French Sorrell Soup, 61
French trim lamb, 113
Fried Chicken, 110
Frittata, 179
frosting, icing, 182

G

Ganache, Chocolate, 139, 164, 182
Gazpacho Soup, Chunky, 62
Galette, Lee's Raspberry, 132
German Potato Salad, Classic, 36
GF, 181
Ginger Soy Dipping Sauce, 29
Gingerbread People, 157
glaze, 182
Gluten Free Biscuits for Blueberry Cobbler, 133
Gluten Free Buttermilk Biscuits, 80
Gluten Free Pizza Dough, 81
Goat Mac N' Cheese, 89
Granola Bars, Kinch's, 171
Granola, 171
grate, 182
Gravy, 104, 182
Green Chili & Pork Tenderloin Soup, 51
green chili prep, 85
Green Chili Sauce, Janette's, 85
Green Peppercorn Sauce, 115
grill, 182
Grilled Beef Tenderloin, 116
Guacamole, 87

H

Harald's Potato Salad, Cold, 36

Herb Crust, 113
Herbed Crusted Rack of Lamb, 113
Herbed Pesto, 107
Hillbilly Chicken, 109
Hoisin Glaze, 120
Hoisin Turkey Spring Rolls, 28
Holiday Cornbread Stuffing, 68
Hollandaise Sauce, 178
Honey Dijon Vinaigrette, 43
Honey Lemon Caper Shrimp, 30
Horsey Sauce, 118
Hot Yeast Rolls, 79

I

immersion blender, 14, 57, 59, 182
Indian Curry with Chicken, 105
Italian Biscotti, Chocolate Dipped, 166

J

Janette's Green Chili Sauce, 85
Jasmine Rice, 106, 114
Jodie's Watermelon Wedges, 22
julienne, 182

K

Kabocha Squash Soup, Fall, 48
Kale Chips, 25
Kale, Brussels Sprout Salad, 34
Key Lime Pie, 143
Key Lime Frozen Treats, Mini, 144
Kinch's Granola Bars, 171
KitchenAid®, 14,183

L

Lamb:
    Lamb Chops, Asian Glazed, 112
    Lamb Saté, 18
    Lamb, Herbed Crusted Rack, 113
Laura's Dressing, 44
Laura's Peach Chutney, 97
Laura's Red Chili Sauce, 86
Lee's Arugula Watercress Salad, 40
Lee's Cha Cha Sauce, aka Chermoula Sauce, 38
Lee's Raspberry Gallette, 132
Leg of Lamb, Butterflied, 111
Lemon Chiffon Cake, 146
Lemon Curd Filling, 146

Collections from an Aspen Chef
Favorite recipes with options to accommodate your dietary preferences

Lemon Curd, 146, 151
Lemon Dijon Vinaigrette, 35, 45
lemon juicer, 15
Lemon Lime Tart, 147
Lemon Pudding Cake, 148
Lemon Royal Icing, 154, 157, 159
Lentil Soup, Vegan, 60
Linda's Dried Beef Curry, 114
Linzer Cookies, 158

M
Mac n'Cheese, 89
macerate, 183
marinate, 183
Marinated Beets, 34
mark, grill, 183
Masa, Tamales, 84
Mashed Potatoes, 76
medley 183
mélange, 183
melon baller, 15
meringue, 183
Meringue Holiday Mushrooms, 138
Meringue, French, 143
Meringue, Italian, 143
mince, 183
Mini Key Lime Frozen Treats, 144
Mint Sauce, 18, 113
Mint Oregano Sauce, 111
Moroccan Chicken Salad, 38
Mrs. B's Skillet Cornbread, 68
Mustard Sauce, 29
Muffins: See Table of Contents, 169

N
Niçoise Salad with Seared Ahi, 35
Nuoc Cham Sauce 27, 39
nutmeg, whole, 57

O
Oatmeal Cherry Cookies, 156
Olive Oil Pie Crust, 179
Onion Soup, Caramelized, 56
Orange Dijon Vinaigrette, 44

P
Pad Thai Rice Noodles, 39
Pancakes, Blueberry Banana, 172
parchment paper, 15
Parchment Wrapped Halibut, 125
Parchment Wrapped Ruby Red Trout, 123
Parmesan Chips, 42
Parmigiano Reggiano, 10
paste, 183
pastry brushes, 15
Pâte Sucrée, 128, 183
Peach Chutney, Laura's, 97
Peach Crisp, Paonia, 131
Peach Rhubarb Jam, 101
Peach Salsa, 98
Peaches, Paonia Canned, 99
Peanut Butter Frosting, 150, 164
Peanut Butter Torte, 150
Peanut Sauce, 19, 39
Pecan Balls, 162
Pecan Slices, Bernice's, 160
peel & devein shrimp, 183
Penne a la Vodka, 90
pesto, 183
Pickles, Bread & Butter, 96
Pies:
    Apple Tarte Tartin, 128
    Basic Pie Crust, 129, 130
    Granny's Apple Pie, 130
    Key Lime Pie, 143
    Lee's Raspberry Gallette, 132
    Lemon Lime Tart, 147
    Olive Oil Pie Crust, 179
    Pâte Sucrée, 128, 183
    Sour Cherry Pie, 129
    Sweet Pie Crust, 132
Pineapple Banana Oatbran Muffins, 175
Pinto Beans, 51
pit, 183
plastic storage containers, 183
Poached Pears, 149
Polenta, Creamy, 74
Pomegranate Reduction Sauce, 117
Pork:
    Baby Back Ribs w/Hoisin Glaze, 120
    Cuban Braised Pork Butt, 122
    Cumin Crusted Pork Tenderloin, 121
    Pork Purses, 29
    Pork, Slow Cooked, 84
    Pork Tenderloin & Green Chili Soup, 51
Port Wine Reduction Sauce, 116
Potato Fries, Baked, 76

Collections from an Aspen Chef
Favorite recipes with options to accommodate your dietary preferences

Potato Leek Soup, 59
Potatoes, Mashed, Vegan, 76
Press'n Seal®, 15
pressure cook, 15, 51,183
Primavera Sauce, 91
Prime Rib w/ Au Jus, 118
pulse, 183
Pumpernickel Toast Points, 23
purée, 183
Puréed Carrot Ginger Soup, 57

Q

Quinoa Mélange, 73
Quiche, 179

R

Ramekin, 183
Raspberry Basil Vinaigrette, 45
Raspberry Coulis Sauce, 147
Raspberry Gallette, Lee's, 132
Raspberry Lemon Trifle, 151
Red Chili Paste, Thai, 106
Red Chili Sauce, Laura's, 86
Red Curry Paste, Thai Kitchen 10
Red Curry, Thai, 106
Reduction Sauce, 183
Remoulade, 183
rhubarb, 101
Ribollita Soup, 58
Roasted Brussels Sprouts, 66
Roasted Cauliflower, 75
Roasted Fennel & Apples, 75
Roux, 89, 183
Royal Icing, 183
Royal Icing, Lemon, 154,157, 159

S

safe minimum cooking temperatures, 13
Salad Dressings:
    Balsamic, 37
    Black Olive Tapenade Dressing, 35
    Caesar's, 42
    Cashew Lemon Vinaigrette, 34
    Cilantro Vinaigrette, 78
    Cranberry Port Vinaigrette, 41
    Danish Blue Cheese, 43
    Fig Balsamic, 45
    Honey Dijon Vinaigrette, 43
    Laura's Dressing, 44
    Lemon Dijon Vinaigrette, 45
    Orange Dion Vinaigrette, 44
    Pomegranate Vinaigrette, 43
    Raspberry Basil Vinaigrette, 45
    Simple Vinaigrette, 38
    Yellow Miso & Bragg Vinaigrette, 44
Salads: See Table of Contents, 34-45
Salmon, Cherry Chipotle Glazed, 124
Sally's Famous Scone Balls, 177
Saté Beef, 18
Saté Chicken, 19
Saté Lamb, 18
Sauces:
    Au Jus, 118
    Black Olive Tapenade, 35
    Cajun Dipping Sauce, 24
    Chermoula Sauce, 38
    Creole Mustard Sauce, 23
    Enchilada Sauce, 88
    Fig Reduction Sauce, 31
    Ginger Soy Dipping Sauce, 29
    Green Chili Sauce, Janette's, 85
    Green Peppercorn Sauce, 115
    Hoisin Glaze, 120
    Mint Sauce, 18, 113
    Mint Oregano Pesto Sauce, 111
    Mustard Sauce, 29
    Nuoc Chom Sauce, 27, 39
    Peanut Sauce, 19, 39
    Pomegranate Reduction Sauce, 117
    Port Wine Reduction Sauce, 116
    Primavera Sauce, 91
    Raspberry Coulis, 147
    Red Chili Sauce, Laura's, 86
    Spicy Chili Aioli Sauce, 20
    Tequila Lime Dipping Sauce, 22
sauté, 184
Sautéed Zucchini, 73
scald, 184
Scones, Sally's Famous, 177
Seal-a-Meal®, 14
sear, 184
Seven Minute Icing, 146
sheet pans, 14
shred, 184
Shredded Chicken, Pressure Cooked, 85
Shrimp:
    Grilled Creole Shrimp, 24

Collections from an Aspen Chef
Favorite recipes with options to accommodate your dietary preferences

    Grilled Shrimp on Vietnamese Salad, 39
    Honey Lemon Caper Shrimp, Grilled, 30
    Shrimp Ceviche, Southwestern, 21
Shortbread Crust, 165
Side Dishes: See Table of Contents, 66-81
simmer, 184
Simple Vinaigrette, 38
skewer, 184
Skillet Cornbread, Mrs. B's, 68
Slow Cooked Pork, 84
Sorrel Soup, 61
soup wand, 57, 59
Soups: See Table of Contents, 48-63
Sour Cherry Pie, 129
Sour Chery Preserves, 100
Southwestern Corn Salad, 78
Southwestern Cornbread, 67
Southwestern Crab cakes, 20
Southwestern Shrimp Ceviche, 21
Spaghetti Carbonara, 92
Spelt Risotto, Farrotto, 71
Spicy Sprouted Beans, 74
Split Pea Soup, 63
Spring Rolls:
    Hoisin Turkey Spring Rolls, 28
    Duck & Shrimp Spring Rolls, 27
stand mixer, 14
Steak au Poivre, 115
Steak, Blackened, 93
Sterilizing Jars, 96
stock, 184
strain, 184
Stuffed Pasta Shells, Tofu, 91
Sugar Cookies, Holiday, 159
sweat, 184
Sweating Eggplants, 91
Sweet Pie Crust, 132
Sweet Potato Fries, 76

T
Tapenade, Black Olive, 35
Tequila Cured Salmon, 23
Tequila Lime Dipping Sauce, 22
Texas Style Pinto Beans, Charra, 70
Thai Red Chili Paste, 106
Thai Red Curry, 106
Toast Points, Pumpernickel, 23
Toasted Pine nuts, 73
Tofu Stuffed Pasta Shells, 91

Tucson Soup, Ribollita, 58
Turkey, Oven Roasted, 104

U
US Weights & Measures, 13

V
Vegan Cheesecake, 140
Vegan Chili, 54
Vegan Chocolate Mousse, 134
Vegan Cream Cheese Frosting, 135, 176
Vegan Lentil Soup, 60
Vegan Whipped Frosting, 140
Vegetarian Enchiladas, 88
Veggie Burgers, 77
VG, 181
Vietnamese Chicken & Shrimp Salad, 39
vinaigrette, 184

W
Waffles, Corn Grit, 173
Watermelon Wedges, 22
whip, 184
whisk, 184
Wild Rice Pilaf, 72
Will's Brine, Turkey, 104

Y
Yellow Miso Bragg Vinaigrette, 44
Yule, Log Cake, 139

Z
zester, 184

Collections from an Aspen Chef
Favorite recipes with options to accommodate your dietary preferences

Acknowledgments
Thank you…

To all of my friends, family and clients who have supported me in my lifetime of cooking, I couldn't have done it without you! Thank you for allowing me to do what I love doing…creating delicious flavorful food with experimenting, trials, and errors. Thank you for enduring endless taste-tests until I got it right!

Mark Batmale, aka "Batman," for your motivation and inspiration with visualizing the writing process and completion of this cookbook. I wouldn't have written or finished this book without your unconditional support, caring attention to detail, and during the process reminding me to take time to enjoy life. Thank you for loving my food, whether it's a simple salad or an elaborate feast.

The late Bonnie Rayburn, for opening me up to the wonderful world of food, and igniting my passion for cooking. She invited me in to share her kitchen at Bonnie's Restaurant with a handful of wonderfully talented women who became friends for life.

My many editors and proofreaders, "Foodies" and a Cordon Bleu Chef. I never imagined how many of my friends were English majors and English teachers. You all went above and beyond, spending countless hours on editing and proofreading. I thank you for your friendship and support! Thank you Frances Pearce, Janette Logan, Carolee Murray, Mark Batmale, Sallyanne Johnson, Dianne Madsen, aka "Di Baby", Eileen Rodenhizer, Jan McCoy, Linda Lynch, Jim Albert. Thank you Pat Conway for your awesome editing and finding time to fit me in, during the final stage of my book. Thank you to The Glenwood Springs Writers Workshop for including me in your workshop and sharing your editing ideas. And to Suzanne Clark for your patience with weaving your way through the first draft and enlightening me about cookbook editing terms and rules, you are a saint!

My dad, Irv Rogers, for introducing me to 5 star restaurants at a young age, opening up my palette to exciting new flavors. To my late sweet baby brother David. I loved making you happy with food, you were my biggest fan.

To everyone who shared their recipes with me: Laura Wait for being an amazing chef and influencing me with her spicy inclinations, including Red Chili Sauce and Peach Chutney. Janette Logan for her love of New Mexican food and Green Chili Sauce. Di Baby Madsen for her tasty Vegan Chili. Sallyanne Johnson for her French Sorrel Soup. Irv Rogers (dad) for his yummy beef chili. Cheri Oates for her Aspen famous Banana Nut Bread. Will Frothingham for his scrumptious Will's Turkey Brine. Jodie Bay for her Tequilla Watermelon Wedges. Linda Lynch for her Dry Beef Rub and an education with Thai cuisine. Sally Pierre for her yummy scones. Cary Grief for sharing Aunt Libby's Bourbon Balls, it was a family secret until now. Bernice Hansen for her Pecan Slices.

Collections from an Aspen Chef
Favorite recipes with options to accommodate your dietary preferences

Lee Keating for her healthy rendition of a Waldorf salad. Marcie Musser for her idea of cooking quinoa in carrot juice and her suggestions with grains. And Bonnie Rayburn for her endless amount of solutions and advice on cooking and recipes.

Brigitte Birrfelder and Teddy Lawrence for being my favorite chefs to work with and bounce recipe ideas off of.

Alan Roberts and Tammie Lane for your art consulting on my illustrations and book design.

Jeannie Weinkle and Charlie Saylor for taking the time to share their ideas on Self-Publishing. What a big world it is out there.

To the house managers, kitchen help, servers and bartenders who made it all happen so seemingly effortless. Thank you for making me look good! Sels Mellick and Nancy Schultz for your endless fun and laughter in the kitchen and for your life saving taste-testing guidance. Claudia Arcena for all your help over the years in the kitchen and being able to divert disasters so un-noticeably quick. Shelley Coulombe for taking charge of serving and being able to laugh at our "Doggie Catering" escapades. Sue Schimmenti for being an amazing breakfast chef! Fronk Smith, for being all around awesome and doing everything it takes to get the job done. Joe Brown for being the best bartender in Aspen, Missy Camins, Paula Sahr and Kris Elice for your help way back when.

To Epicurious and Butcher' Block, my favorite specialty food stores and the wonderful people who took care of me: Chris, JD, Will, Lynn, and Jim and all the staff at BB.

To Ross Douglass, Linda Haneck and Linda Lynch for putting my body back together and keeping it strong. To Lisa Wilson for her gifted coaching.

Eileen Rodenhizer for her endless support and reference material in guiding me towards my end product. And introducing me to the best lemon juicer in my collection.

And to my dear Aunt Lydia, who kindly took care of my brother and me when we were young. She would let me help in the kitchen while she made tamales, pickles, thanksgiving dinner, etc. I don't think she realizes how much of an impact she made on me in my youth. Love you Aunt Lydia.

And finally I want to thank all of my wonderful catering clients who've allowed me to cook for their family and friends throughout the years. What a blessing you have been.

Thank you!
XO Cindy

Authors Bio

Cindy Rogers moved to Aspen at the age of eighteen. It was love at first sight. She left for a few years to finish her BFA in Illustration in Southern California, then moved back at twenty-six and has been here ever since. Cindy has been a private chef in Aspen for over thirty years. She loves the outdoors, hiking, skiing, and biking. Cindy makes a living doing both of her passions, as a chef in the winter and an artist in the summer.

www.ingramcontent.com/pod-product-compliance
Lightning Source LLC
Chambersburg PA
CBHW061928290426
44113CB00024B/2840